The

Big

Questions

Earle J. Chute

Copyright © 2021 by Earle J. Chute
All rights reserved

Dedicated to my two best friends,
Barry Bouchillon and Thomas Weakley,
who are always asking me about
the big questions of life.

Statement about the Articles:

These articles are the result of years of fielding the big questions presented by college students throughout the years of my personal ministry. They are my best attempt to answer some of the difficult questions of life that confront us. These answers are found in the bible, which answers all of our questions about life.

All Scripture taken from the NEW AMERICAN STANDARD BIBLE®, Copyright © 1960, 1962, 1963, 1968, 1971, 1973, 1975, 1977, 1995 by The Lockman Foundation. Used by permission. www.Lockman.org

The Table of Contents

1. How to be filled with the Holy Spirit?
2. How can you know the will of God?
3. How can you overcome temptation?
4. How to say no, when lust says yes?
5. How do you shepherd the flock of God?
6. Is Jesus the only way to God?
7. Is the Bible the Word of God?
8. Is there life after death?
9. Is there really such a thing as miracles?
10. Was Jesus really resurrected from the dead?
11. What about all the other religions?
12. What about women?
13. What happened to the dinosaurs?
14. What is a real man?
15. What is the gift of singleness?
16. What is the meaning and purpose of life?
17. What is the sovereignty of God?
18. When will Jesus return?
19. Why are there so many hypocrites in the church?
20. Why do bad things happen to good people?
21. Why is there evil and suffering in the world?

Chapter 1

The Big Question
How to be Filled with the Holy Spirit?

As a young boy I really enjoyed playing Boys' Club football. I was rather short for my age and very stocky. My friends called me "tank." I played many different positions, but my favorites were fullback and middle linebacker.

    I can remember one-night dreaming about playing football in the NFL. My hero was Earl Campbell. He played the big, bruising ball carrier role for the Houston Oilers. He was number 34. We had a lot in common in my dream. We both played football. We both played fullback. We both wore number 34. And we both had the same first name.

    In my dream I put on his jersey and stepped into the backfield of the Oilers. My number was called. I took the hand-off and hit the hole with all the speed I could muster. There was a loud thud as several hundred pounds of defensive lineman landed on my head knocking me several feet in the air. The ball flew from my hands as I was jerked to a sudden stop by the Astroturf. Mercifully, I woke up from my dream with all my bones intact.

What went wrong? We had so much in common; the jersey, the position, even the name. The problem was I wasn't Earl Campbell. I didn't possess the power that he possessed. I was only a shell, a facsimile of the real thing. I had the label but not the reality.

Unfortunately, this is the same situation for most Christians. They are trying to live the Christian life through their own power. They are going through the right motions. They have all the right moves, even the right "uniform," but they are powerless, defeated, and frustrated. They are constantly being knocked backwards and fumbling the ball.

God has provided every disciple with a power source, a <u>dunamis</u> within them. This power comes from above, but abides in the heart of every Christian. It is the power of the Holy Spirit.

In John 14:17 Jesus refers to *"the Spirit of truth, whom the world cannot receive, because it does not behold Him or know Him, but you know*

Him because He abides with you, and will be in you." This was the promise of the indwelling Spirit.

At the point of salvation every Christian receives the Holy Spirit. Such passages as 1 Corinthians 3:16, 6:19, 12:13; and Romans 8:9 confirm this point. However, although the Holy Spirit resides in every Christian, He doesn't always preside over every Christian. Someone once said that although He is <u>resident</u> in every Christian, He is not always <u>president</u> in every Christian.

How can Christ's disciple be filled with this power? By examining Ephesians 5:18 and other related passages we come to the answer.

"And do not get drunk with wine, for that is dissipation, but be filled with the Spirit" (*Ephesians 5:18*).

With these words Paul has described what is to be the normal Christian life for every Christian. Today, however, there is much confusion over the doctrine of the Holy Spirit. The facts are often neglected, distorted, or deliberately misinterpreted. The power of the Holy Spirit is our strength to live the obedient, Christ-like life. Apart from the filling of the Spirit, the Christian life is impossible to live. It becomes a life of self-effort, of grinding it out, of guilt and of frustration. We must be filled with the Spirit.

What does it mean to be filled with the Spirit? This passage explains a contrast, a command, and the consequences of being filled.

The Contrast

"And do not get drunk with wine, for that is dissipation." All people like to be happy and exhilarated. This happiness is often sought by artificial means. It is estimated that today in America there are seven million alcoholics. Millions of others have turned to drugs. These artificial means have destroyed the lives and families of untold numbers.

The early Christians were accused, themselves, of being drunk with wine (*Acts 2:4, 12-13*). It was said of John the Baptist that, *"He will drink no wine or liquor; and he will be filled with the Holy Spirit, while yet in his mother's womb"* (*Luke 1:15*).

Why does Paul make a contrast with being drunk with wine and the filling of the Spirit? A drunk person is different than a sober person. He speaks differently. He walks differently. He acts differently. One who is filled with the Spirit is also a different person. He also speaks, walks and acts differently.

How does one stay drunk? To stay drunk, one must keep drinking. Just because you are drunk one day doesn't guarantee you'll be drunk the next. You must keep drinking.

The Command

Next, we have the command of Paul. He says, *"Be filled with the Spirit."* The word "filled" is pleroo. It means to fill up, to cause to abound, to pervade, to control, to furnish or supply liberally, to flood, to diffuse throughout, to take possession of.

Whatever fills your life will also control your life. If you are full of wine, you'll be controlled by wine. If you are full of anger, you'll be controlled by anger. If you are full of lust, you'll be controlled by lust. If you are full of the Spirit, you'll be controlled by the Spirit. So, the word "filled" implies control and empowerment.

The word "filled" is in the present tense. A moment-by-moment filling is required. We are "right now" to be filled with the Spirit. It is also in the imperative. It is a command to all believers everywhere in any culture and in all ages.

It is in the passive voice. The subject is being acted upon by an outside agent. The Holy Spirit fills the Christian. It is not the result of our begging, pleading, or sincerity. How then are we filled with the Spirit?

"Now on the last day, the great day of the feast, Jesus stood and cried out, saying, 'If any man is thirsty, let him come to Me and drink. He who believes in Me, the Scripture said, 'From his innermost being shall flow rivers of living water.' By this He spoke of the Spirit, whom those who believed in Him were to receive; for the Spirit was not yet given, because Jesus was not yet glorified" (*John 7:37-39*).

Thirst

In this passage we see the two basic conditions for filling: thirst and trust. In verse 37 we see that we must thirst for His control. We must desire it with all our heart. This involves putting aside any known sin, laying aside our own selfish desires, and putting Christ first in our lives.

There must be a confession and forsaking of any known sin.

Romans 12:1-2 describes the necessary attitude of the heart. *"I urge you therefore, brethren, by the mercies of God, to present your bodies a living and holy sacrifice, acceptable to God, which is your spiritual service of worship. And do not be conformed to this world, but be transformed by the renewing of your mind, that you may prove what the will of God is, that which is good and acceptable and perfect."*

Trust

Trust is the second necessary condition. In John 7:38 Jesus says, *"He who believes in Me."* Paul said in Colossians 2:6, *"As you, therefore, have received Christ Jesus the Lord, so walk in Him."* The filling of the Spirit involves faith. We must trust Christ to fill us.

Faith must always have an object. The Christian's faith is in the Word of God. In Ephesians 5:18 we are commanded to be filled. In 1 John 5:14-15 we have the promise that, *"If we ask anything according to His will, He hears us. And if we know that He hears us in whatever we ask, we know that we have the requests which we have asked from Him."*

Since we know it's God's will for us to be filled, if we ask in faith, we can know that He will fill us. His filling is a direct result of our faith in His word.

Therefore, a prayer for His filling would involve both an expression of our desire to be filled and an expression of our trust in Jesus to do it.

As a disciple we must be filled with the Spirit. Are you filled right now? If not, you can be. Does this prayer express the desire of your heart?

"Lord Jesus, I desire to be filled with your Spirit. I ask you to be the center of my life. I trust you right now to fill me with your Holy Spirit as you have commanded me to do. Thank you for filling me with your Spirit. Amen."

The Consequences

What are the consequences of being filled with the Spirit? Let me mention five major results:

1. <u>Spiritual Fruit</u>. Galatians 5:22-23 says, *"But the fruit of the Spirit is love, joy, peace, patience, kindness, goodness, faithfulness, gentleness, self-control."*
2. <u>Singing</u>. There will be a song in our heart. Ephesians 5:19 says, *"Speaking to one another in Psalms and hymns and spiritual songs, singing and making melody with your heart to the Lord."*
3. <u>Saying Thanks</u>. We will have a heart of thanksgiving and gratefulness. Ephesians 5:20 says, *"Always giving thanks for all things in the name of our Lord Jesus Christ to God, even the Father."*
4. <u>Submitting to One Another</u>. Ephesians 5:21-6:9 describes a submission of life that applies to all of our relationships with others. This is reflective of a humble servant's heart towards God and one another.
5. <u>Spiritual Victory</u>. There will be greater victory in our struggle against sin and Satan as we put on the full armor of God (*Ephesians 6:10-20*).

"Dear Lord Jesus. I come to you today as a humble servant; broken and contrite. I confess to you my sin, my self-centeredness, and my self-dependence. I invite you today to be the very center of my life. I ask you to be the Lord of my life. I ask you by faith to fill me with your Holy Spirit. Thank you for hearing and answering my prayer. In Jesus name. Amen.

Chapter 2

The Big Question
How Can you know the Will of God?

"God loves you and offers a wonderful plan for your life?" What do those familiar words mean? Does God have a plan for me? Is his plan wonderful? Is it free of pain, worry, fear, and doubt? Is there a clear path for my life that God wants to show me? Why is finding God's will for my life so difficult to discover? Is God like a cosmic Easter bunny, who has hidden the golden egg of his will in the bushes?

    I would like to start to answer this question by asking another question: "Are you willing to do God's will when you discover it?" Here is what Jesus said about this in John 7:17, *"If anyone is **willing** to do His will, he will know of the teaching, whether it is of God or whether I speak from Myself."* Sometimes I wonder if God doesn't reveal His will to us, because He knows that we simply are not willing to do it.

    I am making a difference here between the

revealed and unrevealed will of God. Let me say clearly and boldly that the will of God is ALWAYS consistent with the Scriptures. It never contradicts. The revealed will of God is found in the Scriptures. The unrevealed will of God is the will of God outside of the direction of specific Scriptures. (for example: Who to pick for a mate. What job to take. What major to choose in college. What color car to buy. The specific answer to these questions and similar questions are not found in the Bible.)

However, here are some Scriptures that **clearly** reveal to us what is God's will for our lives:

1) Salvation—2 Peter 3:9 *"not **wishing** for any to perish but for all to come to repentance"*; 1 Timothy 2:4 *"who **desires** all men to be saved and to come to the knowledge of the truth"*

2) Sanctification—1 Thessalonians 4:3 *"for **this is the will of God**, your sanctification; that is, that you abstain from sexual immorality"*

3) Suffering—1 Peter 4:19 *"those who suffer according to **the will of God**"*

4) Submission—1 Peter 2:13-15 *"submit yourselves for the Lord's sake...for such is **the will of God.**"*

5) Spirit filled life—Ephesians 5:17-18 *"So then do not be foolish, but understand what **the will of the Lord** is. And do not get drunk with wine, for that is dissipation, but be filled with the Spirit"*

The problem is not finding God's will. The problem is that we choose not to obey his revealed will. The first step in finding the unrevealed will of God for your life is doing the revealed will of God for your life. I'd start with the five things I just mentioned above.

But for the unrevealed will of God for your life, let me suggest that you work through the following questions:

Here are five questions to ask as you determine to discern God's will for your life. They help form principles of wise decision making:

1. What does God's Word say that applies as a principle to my situation?

(A principle is a timeless, cultureless thread throughout Scripture, usually demonstrated by Jesus, explained in the Epistles, and is never contrary to God's Word. 2 Timothy 3:16-17; Hebrews 4:12-13; Psalm 119:105)

2. What do Wise Counselors say about my decision?

God can use the wisdom of godly men and women who know you well to help you with your decision. (Proverbs 11:14; 12:15; 15:31-33)

To choose a wise counselor consider:
- Someone who knows you well—gifts, strengths, weaknesses.
- Someone who walks with God and knows the ways of God.
- Someone who is informed on what God is doing in the world.
- Someone who will be objective with you.

3. Are you Seeking the will of God through Prayer?

   Prayer is aligning our will with the will of God. (James 1:5-6; Proverbs 3:5-6)

4. Are you using your God-given Sound Mind?

   The "call of God' is the calm, inward, persistent sense that you should go! (2 Timothy 1:7; 1 Corinthians 2:14-16)

   Here are some examples where the Apostles used their sound minds to determine God's will: 1Thessalonians 3:1-2--"we thought it best" Philippians 2:25-26--"I thought it necessary"
   I Corinthians 16:3-4--"if it is fitting"
   Acts 6:2-4--"it is not desirable"
   Acts 15:28-29--"it seemed good"

   Another way to use the sound mind principle is to create a Pro-Con list. On a sheet of paper write out all the pros and cons for your situation. Ask which of the points on your list has the most "weight" or "importance" to you? Which choice seems like the best choice for you? Which brings the most glory to God? Are any of the choices contrary to Scripture? Is it merely a matter of preference?

Pro	Con
1.	1.
2.	2.
3.	3.
4.	4.

5. Are you willing to step out in Faith and Trust in the character of God to direct your steps and cover for your mistakes?

   Faith is not waiting until you are 100% sure! That's why it's called Faith!!! (Psalm 32:8-9; 37:4-5)
   How can you be 100% sure of anything? Do you know the infinite mind of God that well?
   Psalm 32:8-9 *"I will instruct you and teach you in the way which you should go; I will*

counsel you with My eye upon you. Do not be as the horse or mule which have no understanding, whose trap-pings include bit and bridle to hold them in check."

Horse: tends to run ahead
Mule: tends to lag behind

In your decision making are you more like the horse or the mule? Do you tend to "run ahead" of God's will? Or do you tend to "lag behind" God's will? I'd suggest a center ground. Strive to always be in the center of God's will.
Psalm 37:4-5 *"Delight yourself in the Lord; and He will give you the desires of your heart. Commit your way to the Lord, trust also in Him, and He will do it."*
Ask: "What do you want to do?" As you have delighted in the Lord and committed yourself to His ways, what desires has He laid upon your heart? Choose to do His will.

Three Subjective Caution Signs:

These are helpful, but not authoritative. I would use great caution in basing a decision on purely subjective means. I am always fearful when someone says, "The Lord told me to do this or to say this." How do you know it was the Lord? If it's based entirely on the subjective, can you really know for sure?

1. The Peace of God

Colossians 3:15 has nothing to do with decision making. What is the source of the peace? A hassle-free life or the Lord? Peace often comes after a faith decision. False peace may come because you made any decision! However, God can fill you with His peace to confirm His will.

2. The Open Door/Closed Door method

How do you discern the difference? Ex: Red Sea for Moses, an apparent closed door. Acts 16:6 how did the Holy Spirit "forbid" Paul? Does an open door mean it's God's will? Ex: Jonah finding a boat to Tarshish. The door was wide open for

Jonah to flee from God's will. Sometimes God wants us to resist walking through the open door or to forcefully enter through the closed door.

3. Impressions

What is an impression? Does God always give an impression? No. Is it God's voice, Satan's voice, or my own desires? All impressions must be tested by the Word of God and Wise counsel. God **never** acts contrary to His Word! However, God can you give you deep impressions that confirm His will. Are we listening to the "still, small, gentle voice of God?"

<u>**For further thoughts on Discerning the Will of God, work through the following Agree/Disagree statements and the case studies.**</u>

Agree or Disagree with the following statements:

**It is impossible to miss out on God's will for my life if my heart is right before Him.

**God's will is not a person, time, or place but rather a relationship with Him.

**It is not possible for a Christian to marry the "wrong" person or choose the "wrong" career path.

Discuss the Case Study:
Bob is a believer at East Tennessee State University. He had met Linda, a girl in his class and was convinced that Linda was for him. After all she was beautiful, smart, and very outgoing. He was a bit uncomfortable that she was not a believer, but they really loved each other. Bob was convinced that she would become a believer later. Bob had sought the counsel from his parents and high school buddies and they had all given the "green light" to get married. He is now coming to you to ask your opinion on God's will for his life. What would you tell him?

Meagan is a believer at Clemson. When she was a teenager, she felt she had "received the call" to the mission field while attending a revival at her church. She went forward at the invitation of the Pastor. She had planned her whole life to go to the mission field after graduation from college. Now as a graduating Senior she has been offered a very high paying job with a local company with lots of benefits, health insurance, and opportunity for travel and advancement. Her best friends are telling her to take the job and that she would be crazy not to. What will you tell her to do?

Chapter 3

The Big Question
How can you Overcome Temptation?

What is temptation? (It is not just the name of the singing group from the '60s.) Temptation is an enticement to evil. Temptation is an enticement to sin. Temptation is an enticement to turn us away from God.

Temptation is different than trials or testings. Temptations are an enticement to evil. God NEVER tempts anyone. God never entices any one to evil. Trials and testings are different. Trials and testings are for our approval. They prove that we "pass the test." God does bring trials and testings into our lives.

Job is a perfect example of this. Job was a righteous man who walked with God. God allowed trials and testings into his life to "prove" his faith in God. His faith was tested, but in the test his faith was made more pure. Job passed the test.

We can see this distinction in the book of

James: *"Blessed is a man who perseveres under trial; for once he has been <u>approved</u>, he will receive the crown of life which the Lord has promised to those who love Him. Let no one say when he is <u>tempted</u>, "I am being tempted by God"; for God cannot be tempted by evil, and He Himself does not tempt anyone. But each one is tempted when he is carried away and <u>enticed</u> by his own lust. Then when lust has conceived, it gives birth to sin; and when sin is accomplished, it brings forth death."* (James 1:12-15)

In this passage, I have underlined the words, "approved," "tempted," and "enticed." I will try to define each of those words.

The word "approved" in verse 12 is the Greek word, <u>dokimos</u>. This word means tried and true, tested, approved. It has the meaning of approval. Testings and trials are for our approval. They prove that our faith is genuine. In the first century this word was connected to the genuine weight of the minted coins. This is what Donald Barnhouse says of this situation. "But some money changers were men of integrity who would accept no counterfeit money. They were men of honor who put only genuine full weighted money into circulation. Such men were called "dokimos" or "approved."[1]

In verse 13 we find the word, "tempted." The Greek word is <u>peirazo</u>. This word means to try or attempt. In the context of this verse, it meant an enticement to evil. God never tempts anyone.

In verse 14 we find the word, "enticed." This word in the Greek is <u>deleazo</u>. This word means to bait, to lure, to lure by using bait, to entice, to seduce, to catch by a bait. The person being tempted is "enticed by his own lust." In other words, his own lust is drawing him away from God. Our flesh provides the "bait" to lure us away from God.

I love to fish. When I was a kid, I fished all the time with my brothers and friends in the Potomac River. (At that time, it was very polluted. Now it is pretty cleaned up.) We would camp out on the river and rise up early in the morning. We

---

[1] Strong, J. (1996). *The exhaustive concordance of the Bible : Showing every word of the text of the common English version of the canonical books, and every occurrence of each word in regular order.* (electronic ed.). Ontario: Woodside Bible Fellowship

had a tackle box full of our lures and bait. We would select a lure or bait that would work to catch fish. We had lures for all occasions. Lures that worked on sunny days. Lures that worked on cloudy days. Lures for cold weather. Lures for warm weather. The lures were different colors, shapes, and weights. The lures were all different, but they all had one common purpose. The purpose of the lure was to catch fish. The lure would entice the fish to take the bait in its mouth. When it did, it was hooked.

Temptation is very similar to the lures in my tackle box. Our enemy, the devil, has his own tackle box with my name on it. He knows exactly what lure would most tempt me in the moment. He knows what lure to use. He knows when to use it. He knows how to dangle it in front of my nose. He knows how to tempt me most effectively.

But we have hope. It is possible to resist temptation. The devil is not all powerful or all knowing. He is not God.

Paul says in 1 Corinthians 10:13, *"No temptation has overtaken you but such as is common to man; and God is faithful, who will not allow you to be tempted beyond what you are able, but with the temptation will provide the way of escape also, so that you will be able to endure it."*

In this statement several things become clear about temptation. First, we see that temptations are "common" to man. We are all tempted. If you are a man, you will be tempted. Your personal temptation is not unique. The precise temptation may be unique, but the essence of the temptation is not new.

There are three basic sources of temptation: the world, the flesh, and the devil. John says this in 1 John 2:15-17, *"Do not love the world nor the things in the world. If anyone loves the world, the love of the Father is not in him. For all that is in the world, the lust of the flesh and the lust of the eyes and the boastful pride of life, is not from the Father, but is from the world. The world is passing away, and also its lusts; but the one who does the will of God lives forever."*

We are tempted by the lust of the flesh, the lust of the eyes, and by the boastful pride of life. These are the same three things that Adam and Eve were tempted by in the garden. *"When the woman saw that the tree was good for food, and that it was a delight to the eyes, and that the tree was desirable to make one wise, she took from its fruit and ate; and she gave also to her husband with her, and he ate."* (Genesis 3:6) The tree was "good for food"—the flesh. The tree was "a delight to the eyes"—the eyes. The tree was "desirable to make one wise"—the pride of life. The same three things could be illustrated by the wilderness temptation of Jesus. (Matthew 4:1-11)

All temptation is common to man. God is always faithful. We are all tempted. There is no exception. No one reaches a "spiritual nirvana," where you are no longer tempted. We are never tempted beyond our capacity to resist. There is always a way out of the temptation. God will always provide a way of escape. Finally, all temptations can be endured. In other words, we can never say I was tempted beyond my ability to resist. We can never say, "The devil made me do it." Every temptation can be resisted. Every sin can be avoided without exception.

So how can we overcome temptation? Let me give you three practical ideas. First, walk with God each day. Saturate your mind and thoughts with the Word of God. Stay filled with the Spirit. Live a life that is filled with prayer. As we walk closely with God, He will give us the strength to resist temptation. Memorize specific Scriptures in your particular area of temptation. For example, if you are tempted by lust, then memorize, 2 Timothy 2:22. *"Now flee from youthful lusts and pursue righteousness, faith, love and peace, with those who call on the Lord from a pure heart."* If you are being tempted by pride, then memorize, James 4:10. *"Humble yourselves in the presence of the Lord, and He will exalt you."*

Secondly, learn to resist the temptation. Different temptations are handled in different ways. Flee youthful lust. Ignore the world. Resist the devil and he will flee. If you are in a situation where you are tempted to lust, then remove yourself from the situation. Turn off the computer. Walk out of the movie. Change the channel. Flee from the tempting situation. If the world is tempting you, learn to ignore the world. Jesus said to be in the world, but not "of" the world. You don't have to retreat to a cave in the mountains. You can turn away from the materialism and greed that the world presents to us. If you feel like the devil is tempting you directly, then claim the blood of Christ over the enemy. Declare him defeated. Resist the devil and he will flee. (Read through Luke 4 to see how Jesus resisted the devil's temptations in the wilderness.)

Finally, be honest about your temptations. Be honest with God. Be aware of where and when your temptations take place. Who are you with? What were you doing? What were you seeing? Some of that may be preventable. Be honest with a trusted friend who can help you stay accountable. Share with your friend how you are doing in your walk with God. Pray together for victory.

In conclusion remember the words of Paul that no temptation is too great or too severe for us to overcome. You can resist temptation. Remember also, that God has forgiven you. If you know Jesus Christ as your Savior and Lord, then you are completely forgiven for all of your sin. He is ready and willing to cleanse us from that sin as we confess it to God. Remember when you do sin that you have an Advocate with the Father!
"My little children, I am writing these things to you

so that you may not sin. And if anyone sins, we have an Advocate with the Father, Jesus Christ the righteous; and He Himself is the propitiation for our sins; and not for ours only, but also for those of the whole world." (1 John 2:1-2)

Overcoming Temptation Worksheet

Today's Sin	The Old West
a. Materialism	___ "I've got the biggest ranch in town."
b. Cheating	___ Train robbery at sundown
c. Lust	___ Mighty nice gun
d. Greed	___ An extra ace in the deck
e. Pride	___ Saloon girls

Why do you sin? Check the four that best apply to you:

[ ] I like the way it feels.
[ ] It is a weak spot for me personally
[ ] I got fooled initially, but now I'm addicted.
[ ] Other people do it all the time.
[ ] I haven't completely surrendered that area to God.
[ ] I lack accountability on the issue.

[ ] I'm not the only one with this problem.
[ ] All of the above.

Define the door to lust for you:
[ ] Entertaining thoughts.
[ ] Second glances and wandering eyes.
[ ] A mouse click on www....
[ ] Cable TV and movies.
[ ] Magazines

Hold me accountable and encourage me by:
[ ] a phone call.
[ ] an email or text message.
[ ] pray for me daily.
[ ] Ask me the following questions when you see me. (Write the questions below):

Winning the Next Battle:
1. Look away. (Job 31:1; Pv 6:25)
2. Read and Know the Word. (Pv 6:23; Eph 6:13-17)
3. Identify your weak moments. (Lk 4:13)
4. Fight on your knees. (Col 3:2)

<u>Between You and God:</u>
1. Thank God for His forgiveness through Christ. (Col 2:14)
2. Lay before Him your greatest temptation. (Mt 6:13)
3. Ask the Holy Spirit to show you:
    a. The chinks in your armor
    b. An escape route. (I Cor 10:13)
    c. The resource of Christ in your Heart. (Gal 2:20)[2]

---

[2] From <u>The Highest Education</u> by Gregg Matte. Chapter 3.

Chapter 4

The Big Question
How to say "No," when lust says "Yes."

We live in a world today where our "word" means very little. We make and break agreements. We break our vows. We often choose the painful path of pleasure over denial. Our wills are soft. We give in so easily to pressure. We can't turn from temptation. We are used to getting our way. We lack moral fiber. We rarely find men and women of integrity. What is the problem? Why is it so hard to say "no," when lust says, "yes."?

      I want to answer this question by looking at a chapter from the life of Joseph. It is found in chapter 39 of the book of Genesis. Spend some time reading it and contemplating its message.

Now Joseph had been taken down to Egypt; and Potiphar, an Egyptian officer of Pharaoh, the captain of the bodyguard, bought him from the

Ishmaelites, who had taken him down there. The LORD was with Joseph, so he became a successful man. And he was in the house of his master, the Egyptian. Now his master saw that the LORD was with him and how the LORD caused all that he did to prosper in his hand. So, Joseph found favor in his sight and became his personal servant; and he made him overseer over his house, and all that he owned he put in his charge. It came about that from the time he made him overseer in his house and over all that he owned, the LORD blessed the Egyptian's house on account of Joseph; thus, the LORD'S blessing was upon all that he owned, in the house and in the field. So, he left everything he owned in Joseph's charge; and with him there he did not concern himself with anything except the food which he ate.

Now Joseph was handsome in form and appearance. It came about after these events that his master's wife looked with desire at Joseph, and she said, "Lie with me." But he refused and said to his master's wife, "Behold, with me here, my master does not concern himself with anything in the house, and he has put all that he owns in my charge. There is no one greater in this house than I, and he has withheld nothing from me except you, because you are his wife. How then could I do this great evil and sin against God?" As she spoke to Joseph day after day, he did not listen to her to lie beside her or be with her. Now it happened one day that he went into the house to do his work, and none of the men of the household was there inside. She caught him by his garment, saying, "Lie with me!" And he left his garment in her hand and fled, and went outside. When she saw that he had left his garment in her hand and had fled outside, she called to the men of her household and said to them, "See, he has brought in a Hebrew to us to make sport of us; he came in to me to lie with me, and I screamed. When he heard that I raised my voice and screamed, he left his garment beside me and fled and went outside." So, she left his garment beside her until his master came home. Then she spoke to him with these words, "The Hebrew slave, whom you brought to us, came in to me to make sport of me; and as I raised my voice and screamed, he left his garment beside me and fled outside."

Now when his master heard the words of his wife, which she spoke to him, saying, "This is what your slave did to me," his anger burned. So, Joseph's master took him and put him into the jail, the place where the king's prisoners were confined; and he was there in the jail. But the LORD was with Joseph and extended kindness to him, and gave him favor in the sight of the chief jailer. The chief jailer committed to Joseph's charge all the prisoners who were in the jail; so that whatever was done there, he was responsible for it. The chief jailer did not supervise anything under Joseph's charge because the LORD was with him; and whatever he did, the LORD made to prosper.

Let me share a little of the back story of the life of Joseph, before we address our big question. Joseph was one of the 12 sons of Israel. He was a dreamer. He wore the multicolored robe. His dreams seemed to lift him up above his father, mother, and brothers. His brothers grew to hate him and became embittered against him. They eventually sell him off into slavery. He ends up through a series of amazing circumstances in

Egypt. Then through another series of amazing circumstances, he ends up in the house of Potiphar, the head of Pharaoh's personal bodyguard. (Read the whole story of Joseph in Genesis 35-50.)

Now the rest of the story. We learn four things about Joseph:

1) He was a successful man. Verse 2 says, *"The Lord was with Joseph, so he became a successful man."* Joseph was a man who could get things done. He had achieved incredible success. He was a leader, a manager, and an administrator. If he was alive today, he would be doing seminars on weekends, teaching on how to be successful.

2) He was a blessed man. Verse 5 says, *"It came about that from the time he made him overseer in his (Potiphar's) office and over all that he owned, the Lord blessed the Egyptian's house on account of Joseph; thus, the Lord's blessing was upon all that he owned, in the house and in the field."* Joseph was blessed of the Lord. The Lord blessed all that Joseph touched. Everything he did resulted in a harvest of blessing.

3) <u>He was a handsome man.</u> Verse 6 says, *"Now Joseph was handsome in form and appearance."* Joseph was a stud. His face would have graced all the glamour magazines. He would have been making beer commercials. He could have been a movie star. Like I've said, he was a stud!

4) <u>He was a godly man.</u> Verse 9 says, *"There is no one greater in this house than I, and he has withheld nothing from me except you, because you are his wife. How then could I do this great evil and sin against God?"* Joseph had a relationship with God. The Lord was in control of his life. He was a man of destiny. He somehow knew that God was using him and placing him in his position of authority. Joseph was repeatedly treated wrongly, yet we see no anger, bitterness, or resentment. He trusted in his God.

In the midst of this context, Joseph is faced with the biggest challenge of his life. If he failed this challenge, it could affect the future of the nation of Israel. There were far reaching, eternal consequences to his challenge. Joseph is tempted morally and sexually by Potiphar's' wife.

She directly invites him to "lie with her." At

this time Joseph was a single man. As noted, he was successful, blessed, and handsome. He was a prime target for an immoral woman's advances. (Not sure if this was a "cougar" situation.) It must have been an extremely strong temptation. Who would know? Why not just this one time? Why not enjoy the moment?

Joseph rejects her advances. Apparently, some time goes by in our story. We read in verse 10 that her advances were "day after day." She was very persistent. She didn't give up easily. Her sights were firmly fixed on Joseph. Isn't that exactly how temptation works? It sets it sights on us and doesn't give up until we give in.

Then our story reaches the critical moment. She makes one final attempt to seduce Joseph. They are alone together in the house. None of the men of the household were at home. She grabs Joseph. He pulls away. She clings to his garments. He runs outside the house leaving his garment in her hands.

Her rejection led to vengeance. She tells a story that Joseph had "made sport" of her. Her husband hears and believes her story. He sees Joseph's garment in her hand. Joseph ends up in prison falsely accused and falsely convicted.

What can we learn from this story that will help us to say "no," when lust says, "yes."? Here are three application points that we may learn from.

1) Realize the consequence of sin. Joseph realized that his sin would be a great sin against God. He realized that if he gave in, then his future leadership would be compromised and his integrity would be compromised. In the bigger story, the future of Israel could have been compromised. (Joseph would later "save" Israel during the seven year worldwide famine.) We need to realize the consequence of giving in to sexual sin. In my wallet I keep a list of things that would happen to me and my family, if I ever committed sexual sin with another woman. Make a list yourself. What would be the personal and ministry consequences of your sexual sin, of violating your vows with your wife?

2) Resist the temptation. Paul gives us some great instruction in 1 Corinthians 10:13: *"No temptation has overtaken you but such as is*

common to man; and God is faithful, who will not allow you to be tempted beyond what you are able, but with the temptation will provide the way of escape also, so that you will be able to endure it." It is always possible to say "no" to temptation. No temptation is too great. We can never say "the devil made me do it." We can endure any and all temptations. We can always say "no." There is always a way of escape!

3) <u>Run from the situation.</u> Sometimes we just need to flee. Sometimes we just need to escape. We need to remove ourselves from the tempting situation or circumstances or person. If the temptation is on your computer, turn it off. If it's a movie, walk out. If it's on your television, change the channel. If it's a person, run. End the relationship. Break up with your girlfriend or boyfriend. Sometimes the best way to say "no" is by running. Remove yourself from the temptation. Let me also say on the positive note that we run from the temptation, but we run towards God. I like how Paul instructed young Timothy in 2 Timothy 2:22, *"Now flee from youthful lusts and pursue righteousness, faith, love*

and peace, with those who call on the Lord from a pure heart." We are to flee lust and pursue after God with others who are pursing after God. Strength comes from calling on the Lord from a pure heart.

Another way to resist temptation is to "make up our minds in advance." Daniel as a young man made up his mind in advance that he would not defile himself. (Daniel 1:8) Job made a covenant with his eyes that he would not gaze upon the virgin. (Job 31:1) Make up your mind in advance that you will say "no" to lustful thoughts, actions, and desires. You may want to consider confiding with a close friend so you can pray through your struggle together. Sometimes two are better than one in our resistance towards temptation. And when two are together the Lord is in your midst. (Matthew 18:20)

So how do we say "no," when lust is saying, "yes?" We realize. We resist. We run. We turn from the temptation to God. A good thing to do is to memorize scripture that directly applies to your situation. Put the scripture on a note card and put it on top of your television, or on the dashboard of your car, or on the mirror in your bathroom. Let the Word of Christ richly dwell within you. (Colossians 3:16) Saturate your mind with God's Word. (Psalm 119:9,11) It's pretty had to sin, when you are contemplating the Word of God. When Jesus was tempted in the wilderness, He used the Word of God to resist the temptations of the devil. (For a more detailed conversation about "How to overcome temptation?" read my essay on that topic.)

Finally, we need to <u>remember</u>. We need to remember when we say "no" to sin, all sin, but especially sexual sin, we are bringing glory to God. We are showing the world that it is possible to live a life of moral purity through the power of the Holy Spirit working through our lives. The purity of our lives is a reflection of the purity and holiness of God. If we do sin, we need to remember that as a believer in Christ, all of our sins are forgiven. (Colossians 2:14). They have all been nailed to the cross. We are forgiven through the blood of Christ.

Just say "no," when lust is saying "yes!"

Chapter 5

The Big Question
How do you Shepherd the Flock of God?

One of the greatest roles of a discipler is that of a shepherd to the flock of God. Jesus in Hebrews 13:20 is called the Great Shepherd of the sheep. King David was a shepherd in his youth. (Psalm 78:70-72) Both Peter and Paul refer to the elders of the church as shepherds. (I Peter 5:1-5; Acts 20:28) Spiritual leaders are shepherds.

In this article a "shepherd" is the servant leader. It could be a local leader, a discipleship group leader, a bible study leader or any other leader in the body of Christ. The shepherd is the leader of his flock. The "flock" refers to believers entrusted to the care of the leader. It may be many or it may be few.

In the Old Testament we learn that there are two types of shepherds. Those who shepherd well and those who are negligent. God has very harsh words for those evil shepherds who lead the flock astray. God is looking for the good shepherds. (Ezekiel 34)

A good shepherd is one who knows his sheep well. In John 10 it says that the sheep would know the shepherd's voice and the shepherd would know each sheep by name. Notice in this passage the contrast between the false shepherd and the true shepherd. Notice also the contrast between the familiar voice and the voice of the stranger.

John 10:1-5

1 "Truly, truly, I say to you, he who does not enter by the door into the fold of the sheep, but climbs up some other way, he is a thief and a robber.
2 "But he who enters by the door is a shepherd of the sheep.
3 "To him the doorkeeper opens, and the sheep hear his voice, and he calls his own sheep by name and leads them out.
4 "When he puts forth all his own, he goes ahead of them, and the sheep follow him because they know his voice.

5 "A stranger they simply will not follow, but will flee from him, because they do not know the voice of strangers."

At night in the fields, often several shepherds would put their flocks together into a sheepfold for safety. At first light the shepherds would each stand at the gate and call out his sheep by name. He would recognize them and they would recognize him. The leader is to know his sheep in such a way.

In the open fields the shepherds would build sheep folds or pens to keep the sheep in safety. There was an open gate for the sheep to pass through. At night the shepherd would lay across that gate. His body would be the gate. Jesus Christ is our good Shepherd. Through His life we have life. He is the door. He is the way, the truth, and the life.

A shepherd plays two primary roles that of protector and provider.

Protector

A shepherd was to protect the sheep entrusted to his care. Part of his equipment was the rod, the staff, and the sling. The rod was a blunt ended piece of thick wood. It was used to protect the sheep from attack from predators. It would be used to keep the lion or bear away from the defenseless sheep. The sling was used to protect the sheep from attack from a distance. The shepherd would keep smooth stones in a bag that he would use to ward off predators that were still a distance away. (David used such a weapon in his defeat of Goliath.) The third piece of equipment was the staff. The staff was a long stick with a "crook" at the end. The crook had a fish hooked shaped end. It was used to pull the sheep out of pits, crevices, or other dangers.

Psalm 23 is a much beloved Psalm. This Psalm has brought much comfort for those sheep who are hurting, who have strayed away, who need protection, who need encouragement, and who need comfort and hope. It is a beautiful picture of how the shepherd would watch over his sheep. Verses 1-3 talk about the provision of the shepherd for his sheep. Verses 4-5 talk about the protection of the shepherd for his sheep. Verse 6 refers to the beautiful future for the sheep. This is a great Psalm to meditate upon and dwell upon.

It helps us to see Jesus as our Shepherd.
Psalm 23:1-6

1 The LORD is my shepherd,
I shall not want.
2 He makes me lie down in green pastures;
He leads me beside quiet waters.
3 He restores my soul;
He guides me in the paths of righteousness
For His name's sake.
4 Even though I walk through the valley of the shadow of death,
I fear no evil, for You are with me;
Your rod and Your staff, they comfort me.
5 You prepare a table before me in the presence of my enemies;
You have anointed my head with oil;
My cup overflows.
6 Surely goodness and lovingkindness will follow me all the days of my life,
And I will dwell in the house of the LORD forever.

Another aspect of protection is the discipline of the sheep. The shepherd would have to train each sheep not to stray from the flock. The shepherd would make a special effort to keep the younger sheep close to his care.

    Now and then a very young lamb would have to be taught not to stray from the shepherd. It sounds harsh, but the shepherd would break the leg of the young lamb so it couldn't stray away. He did this so the young lamb would not stray away and be eaten by predators or become lost and die of thirst or starvation. The shepherd would carry that lamb on his shoulder until the leg was healed. That lamb knew well the voice, the smell, and the hands of that shepherd. It never strayed again from the shepherd. (Psalm 51:8 seems to allude to this.)

    In Acts 20 Paul calls for the elders of Ephesus to meet with him for the final time before his death. Here is part of his admonition in Acts 20:28-31:

28 "Be on guard for yourselves and for all the flock, among which the Holy Spirit has made you overseers, to shepherd the church of God which He purchased with His own blood.
29 "I know that after my departure savage wolves will come in among you, not sparing the flock;
30 and from among your own selves men will

arise, speaking perverse things, to draw away the disciples after them.
31 "Therefore be on the alert, remembering that night and day for a period of three years I did not cease to admonish each one with tears.

Paul warns them that there would be two types of dangers: 1) dangers from outside the body of Christ (the Church) and 2) dangers from within the body of Christ. Both dangers are equally serious. The elders were to be on the alert to carefully protect the flock of God. The shepherd leader is always on the alert for such dangers. The predators were lions, bears, and wolves. Some of the predators were wolves in sheep's clothing.

Provider

The other primary duty of the shepherd was to provide for the sheep. Sheep are not very smart. They must be led to pasture and fresh water. It's possible that sheep could die from thirst or starvation if they aren't led to pasture and water. Sheep often stray away. They are never driven they are always led. The shepherd couldn't eat for the sheep, but he could lead them to the green pasture. Isaiah said in Isaiah 53:6:

6 All of us like sheep have gone astray,
Each of us has turned to his own way;
But the Lord *has caused the iniquity of us all*
To fall on Him.

  We are all sheep that have gone astray. We usually choose to go our own way (away from the direction of God). We need a shepherd to "find us" and point us in the right direction.

  The shepherd would clean the sheep and shear its wool. He would care for their wounds, injuries, and bruises. He would constantly try to insure their health and well-being. Each day he would look over the body of the sheep to groom it, care for it, and provide for it. He would clean off the mud and manure that may have matted in its wool.
  A leader is always responsible for his flock. This means that he would know them by name, he would know their face, he would be attentive to them, and he would care for them, provide for

them, and protect them.

In 1 Peter the apostle mentions that there is a special reward for those who shepherd well. Each of us as leaders has the opportunity to receive that crown. It will be a privilege to lay that crown down at the feet of Jesus.

1 Peter 5:4

And when the Chief Shepherd appears, you will receive the unfading crown of glory.

Summary Principles:
1. <u>Spend time with those entrusted to you.</u>
   Discipleship is much more than a one-hour appointment each week. It is the willingness to impart your very life. It is an availability and eagerness that others can discern.

2. <u>Know them by name.</u>
   A name represents the essence of the person. Go beyond the superficial. Find out their background. What are some of their significant life experiences that have shaped them? What are some significant victories as well as failures? Remember

their birthday and significant occasions.

3. <u>Know their "condition"; how they each are doing.</u>
   How did they become a believer? What were they like before salvation? What are they like now? What were some significant life changes? What are they currently struggling with?

4. <u>Provide for them what they need.</u>
   A young believer needs to know the foundations of their faith. An older believer needs the meat of the Word. Some need comfort. Some need exhortation. Some need discipline. Some need an arm wrapped around their shoulders.

5. <u>Protect them from the enemy.</u>
   What struggles and temptations do they currently face. Bring into the light those temptations. Keep them accountable. Learn how the enemy attacks them and prepare them with Scripture to defend themselves.

6. <u>Discipline and correct those that stray.</u>
We all are "prone to wander". We need people in our lives to keep us on the "straight and narrow". Sometimes this involves discipline and correction. Be a bearer of truth in their lives. Always speak the truth in love. Remember the growth model of grace, truth, and time. (Don't forget the time!)

7. <u>Encourage them.</u>
Encouragement may be one of the greatest ministries that a shepherd can have in the life of his sheep. We live in a very discouraging day and age. There is very little out there that will bring us cheer. Some are so discouraged that they have lost hope. Others have been hardened by the deceitfulness of sin. Learn to encourage your sheep. Do it often.

The Tremendous Need for Shepherds

Today there is a tremendous need for shepherds. This present-day generation of students are hungering for those older (at least a little older than they are) mentors to lead, to challenge, to feed, and to direct them. Maybe this shortage explains why so many sheep have strayed away from Christ and His teachings. Why is there such a shortage of qualified shepherds? Maybe some have been disqualified because of their own sin. Maybe some are discouraged because of previous lack of response. Maybe some are lazy and not wanting the "messy" task of shepherding the sheep. Maybe some are somehow unaware of the need.

    The challenge for today is for God to raise-up shepherds for the flock. The best way to prepare for this task is to study the ways of the Good Shepherd, the Master Shepherd, our Great Shepherd. Become a student of the gospels. Study the ways of the Master. Apply what you learn from Him to your leading of others.

    The day will come when the sheep and goats are separated. Those that shepherd will be called into account. It would be wonderful to hear these words from Christ, "Well done my good and faithful servant.

Discussion Questions:

1. What are some of the ways that a shepherd can know well his flock (believers that are entrusted to your care)?

2. What are some of the dangers that believers face in this world? How can the shepherd prepare the flock to face these dangers?

3. What can the shepherd do in his own heart to prepare to lead the flock? (1 Peter 5:1-5)

Chapter 6

The Big Question
Is Jesus the only way to God?

Why do people ask this question? Some ask out of curiosity. Some ask because they resent Christianity and think it to be narrow-minded and bigoted. Some ask because it is a serious concern and a barrier to their coming to faith in Christ.

Let me begin with some illustrations. When an airline pilot is landing the passenger plane that he is piloting, he narrows his landing choices to a single runway. He doesn't land on the interstate. He doesn't land in a pasture. He doesn't land in the ocean. He lands his plane on the runway assigned to him by the air traffic controller. We would never consider that pilot to be narrow-minded or bigoted by landing on that single run way or by following the instructions of the air traffic controller.

Consider when we are driving our cars down the interstate. We stay on our side of the four-lane highway. We hope (and pray) that everyone stays in their proper lane and travels in the right direction. We never consider those drivers to be narrow-minded or bigoted, because they are traveling in the right direction and in the right lane, (Of course in England the left lane would be the correct lane to drive in.)

    Consider the faculty member who is grading our math exam. There are right answers and wrong answers to each math problem. We want to be graded by the correctness of our answers. We don't want the grade to be determined by how the faculty member felt that day or whether or not they had breakfast. We want them to stick closely   to the principles of mathematics and grade our paper accordingly.   We would never consider that faculty member to be narrow-minded or bigoted, because he graded our math exam on the basis of correct addition or multiplication.

    In these three examples we see that there is much in life that provides very narrow and correct choices. Saying that there is only one correct path does not necessarily make us a bigot or narrow-minded.

    Now what if I were to say that chocolate ice

cream is the best flavor of ice cream in the world. Moreover, that all other flavors should be discontinued. In addition, that I had the power and ability to discontinue or destroy all the other ice cream flavors in the world, now that would be narrow-minded and bigoted. The difference is that choosing your favorite flavor of ice cream is a matter of preference. Choosing the correct runway or interstate highway is a matter of life and death.

What if someone were to say that they had discovered the cure for cancer? Somehow through a scientific discovery they found out the right pattern of genetic code that would eliminate cancer from the world. To be cured from cancer you would have to drink a certain medicine in a certain quantity over a precise number of days. Would that be narrow minded or bigoted to say, that only that one medicine would do? That you would have to drink a specific amount over a specific period of time for the cure to work? Or would those instructions be something that could save the very life of the cancer patient.

Jesus states very clearly in John 14:6 that he is the only way to God. He says, *"I am the way, and the truth, and the life. No one comes to the Father but through me."* There is no mistaking the fact that Jesus is claiming to be the single way to reach God. He is the single runway. He is the single lane of traffic. He is the correct solution. He is the single cure.

In Acts 4:12 Luke records these words, *"There is no other name under heaven by which we must be saved."* Yes, he is stating that Jesus is the ONLY way to reach God.

Now there are some specific reasons why Jesus is the only way to God. I'll explain those in a moment, but one more illustration. This time from the Old Testament. In Exodus we read about the rebellion of Israel in the wilderness. Poisonous serpents are sent into the camp as punishment for their rebellion and pride. The people cry out to God for mercy. God instructs Moses to make a bronze serpent. It is to be placed on his staff and lifted into the air. (The serpent wrapped around the staff would later become the symbol of the medical profession...a serpent on a staff.) When the people would look upon that serpent on that staff they would be cured of their bites and live. God did not instruct the people to gaze at Moses or Aaron. God did not instruct the people to look at the sun, moon, or stars. God did not instruct the people to gaze at their navels. He had very specific instructions. To save your life, gaze at the bronze serpent on the staff of Moses. And those who did were saved.

This Old Testament story is an illustration of what would happen in the New Testament. The problem is that we all have sin that needs forgiving. That is the bite of the serpent. Our sin has separated us from God. We come under the judgment of God because of that sin. Therefore, we must find a cure for our sin problem. The cure is the life of Jesus who hung on the cross. When we set our gaze upon him, we are cured and are saved.

God loves everyone. It doesn't matter what your religious affiliation may be. He loves us all. The Buddhist, the Hindu, the Muslim. His invitation extends to all. He is opening wide his arms to all that will come. His invitation is for *you*.

So why Jesus and not anyone else. Because Jesus was the perfect sacrifice for our sin. He is the only sacrifice for our sins. All other sacrifices were blemished by sin. Jesus lived a life of sinless perfection. He had no sin of his own. He was God incarnate. He was sent from heaven by God our Father to redeem the world of sin. He died on the cross. He was buried. On the third day he was raised. Then he appeared to many witnesses, some who still lived at the time of the writing of the gospels. The tomb was empty and still is. All other religious leaders are still in their tombs, but the tomb of Jesus is empty. He is unique in all of history. History is really His-Story.

Chapter 7

The Big Question
Is the Bible the Word of God?

The Bible (I will be capitalizing "Bible" throughout this article.) is one of the most widely read books in the world. It is beyond doubt one of the most published books in the world. It is also the most translated book in the world. The Bible has been printed in just about every known language of the world. (Wycliffe and other organizations are working hard to complete that task.) It is the most unique book of all history. But why do Christians believe, the Bible is the Word of God?

Before addressing that question, it may be helpful to know a little bit about the Bible. The Bible was written over a 1600-year period. It was written in three different languages: Hebrew, Greek, and Aramaic. It was written by over 40 different authors. The Bible itself is composed of two major parts: the Old Testament and the New Testament.

The Old Testament is composed of 39 separate books. It primarily deals with the period of history from the Creation story to the end of the Babylonian captivity. The Old Testament can be outlined in several ways. The first way is by the style of the 39 books. The first 17 books are historical books. These historical books can be divided into the first five books called the Torah, the Law of Moses, or the Pentateuch. The last 12 historical books being a written record of the history of Israel. The second 5 are poetic books. The final 17 are prophetic. The prophetic books can be divided into major and minor prophets. Major and minor being determined by the size of the book and not by its importance.

Another way to outline the Old Testament is through a timeline of Jewish history. Books can be divided into those describing the period before, during, and after the Babylonian captivity. For example, the prophets were prophets either before, during, or after the captivity. The prophetic books can also be divided by the audience to which the book was written; either to Israel or Judah.

The New Testament can also be outlined in

several ways. There are five historical books: the four gospels and Acts. One prophetic book; Revelations. This leaves us with 21 epistles. Together they total the 27 books of the New Testament. The epistles can be divided up in several ways according to the recipient of the letter. Some letters were written to individuals: Timothy, Titus, Philemon; some to churches in particular cities: Romans, Corinthians, Ephesians, Thessalonians, etc; and some to groups of people: Hebrews. Other epistles are entitled by the author's name; Peter, John, Jude, and James.

An important passage found in 2 Timothy 3:16-17 describes the idea of the "inspiration of the scripture."

"All scripture is inspired by God and profitable for teaching, for reproof, for correction, for training in righteousness; so that the man of God may be adequate, equipped for every good work."

The phrase "inspired by God" in this verse is the Greek word: theopneustos[3]. The word is composed of two Greek words. The first part of

---

[3] Strong, J. (1996). *Enhanced Strong's Lexicon* (G2316). Ontario: Woodside Bible Fellowship.

the word is "theos" which means "god." The second part of the word is "pneo," which means "breath, blow, or wind." So, the Greek word for "inspired" means the breath of God. That is what inspiration means. The Bible describes itself as being the very "breath of God." The words and meaning of the words are inspired by God. This inspiration is different than the inspiration of an artist or composer or poet. Inspiration is the idea that God Himself has inspired the very words of the Bible.

Another important passage is 2 Peter 1:20-21:

"But know this first of all, that no prophecy of Scripture is a matter of one's own interpretation, for no prophecy was ever made by an act of human will, but men moved by the Holy Spirit spoke from God."

The term "moved" by the Holy Spirit describes how the Bible was written. It was written by men, who were moved by the Holy Spirit. The word "moved" is the Greek word: phero[4]. This word means to bring, bear, or bring

---

[4] Strong, J. (1996). *Enhanced Strong's Lexicon* (G5342). Ontario: Woodside Bible Fellowship.

forth. Men are "brought along" to write the scripture. I would compare it to a sailboat at sea. The rudder of the boat controls the direction, but the wind is what fills the sails and pushes the boat along. In other words, the Holy Spirit uses the knowledge, experience, personality, of the writer, but it is the Holy Spirit who inspires him to write. The Bible was not written by "automation" or by a mindless author who simply recorded what was dictated. It was the work of the Holy Spirit through the human author.

Another passage that I would like to refer to is found in Hebrews 4:12:

"For the word of God is living and active and sharper than any two-edged sword, and piercing as far as the division of soul and spirit, of both joints and marrow, and able to judge the thoughts and intentions of the heart."

This passage teaches that the Bible itself is the "word of God." The word of God can look into our hearts and determine our motives, thoughts, attitudes, etc. What other written book can do this?

Another interesting passage that sheds some light on this subject is found in 2 Peter 3:15-

16:
> *"And regard the patience of our Lord as salvation; just as also our beloved brother Paul, according to the wisdom given him, wrote to you, as also in all his letters, speaking in them of these things, in which are some things hard to understand, which the untaught and unstable distort, as they do also the rest of the Scriptures, to their own destruction."*

What is interesting in this passage is that Peter is including Paul's writings in with "the *rest* of the Scriptures." Up to this point, only the Old Testament had been written. The New Testament writers were just beginning to write the New Testament. Peter recognized the inspiration of Paul's letters as the very Word of God.

I do not think anything that I have written so far "proves" that the Bible is the Word of God, but it at least gives you an idea of the composition of the Bible and what it says about itself.

Here are six reasons why I think the Bible is the Word of God:

1) The fulfillment of prophecy proves the Bible is the Word of God. When you study the prophetic

books, it is amazing to see how the prophecies were fulfilled. A prime example of this were the Old Testament prophecies that described the birth, life, death, and burial of Jesus. These prophecies were written many hundreds of years in advance.

2) The unique place of the Bible in human history proves that it is the Word of God. As previously, described, no other book is anything like it.

3) The changed lives of those who have read and applied the Bible prove that it is the Word of God. When you take the Bible and begin to live out its Word, it will change your life.

4) The message of salvation, forgiveness of sins, and eternal life proves that the Bible is the Word of God. Through believing the Bible, we can have our sins forgiven and receive eternal life. No other book will provide that.

5) My own changed life is proof that the Bible is the Word of God. When I began to believe the Bible and apply it to my life as a sophomore in

college it changed my life. I became a believer in Christ as a result of reading the Bible.

6) Archaeological studies help to prove that the Bible is the Word of God. Practically every time a spade goes in the ground in the Middle East there seems to be an additional confirmation of the people, places, and history of the Bible. I would like to offer the following quotes to help establish this argument. They all come from Josh McDowell's excellent book, <u>Evidence that Demands a Verdict</u>.[5]

Nelson Glueck, the renowned Jewish archaeologist, wrote, "It may be stated categorically that no archaeological discovery has ever controverted a biblical reference." [6]

William F. Albright, known for his reputation as one of the great archaeologists, states: "There can be no doubt that archaeology has confirmed the substantial historicity of Old

---

[5] Josh McDowell, *Evidence that Demands a Verdict*, (Here's Life Publishers, 1979), pages 65-66.
[6] Nelson Glueck, *Rivers in the Desert; History of Negev*, (Philadelphia: Jewish Publications Society of America, 1969), page 31.

Testament tradition." [7]

F.F. Bruce notes, "Where Luke has been suspected of inaccuracy, and accuracy has been indicated by some inscriptional evidence, it may be legitimate to say that archaeology has confirmed the New Testament record."[8]

You may be asking why this question is so important. This question is important because if the Bible really is what it claims to be, the Word of God (and I believe that it is); then it has some very important things to say to us. It can show us how to live. It can comfort us in time of sorrow. It can strengthen us in time of weakness. It can show us the future. It can explain to us the pathway to salvation, forgiveness of sins, and eternal life.

The Bible can "scare the hell" out of us. It can calm our fears. It can restore what has been broken. It can find what has been lost. It can change your life.

---

[7] William F. Albright, *Archaeology and the Religions of Israel*, (Baltimore: Johns Hopkins University Press, 1956), page 176.

[8] F.F. Bruce, *Archaeological Confirmation of the New Testament. Revelation and the Bible*. Edited by Carl Henry. (Grand Rapids: Baker Book House, 1969), page 331.

Read the Bible today. Ask God to speak to your heart. A good place to begin is the gospel of John. This gospel was written for a very special reason.

"Therefore, many other signs Jesus also performed in the presence of the disciples, which are not written in this book; but these have been written so that you may believe that Jesus is the Christ, the Son of God, and that believing you may have life in His name." (John 20:30-31)

For more information on this topic read <u>Evidence that Demands a Verdict</u> by Josh McDowell.

Chapter 8

The Big Question
Is there Life after Death?

Remember going on a family vacation? You packed your bags. You had the newspaper held. You made sure the neighbors knew you were leaving. You paid all your bills. You did all that you could to prepare to leave. However, what if you went on a vacation and never came back. What would you have done differently in preparing to go? Are there others you would have said good-bye to? Is there anything else you would have packed? Life is like that. We are all on a journey that eventually finishes with a common ending. Life is full of the unexpected. Life is short. It may come unexpectedly. We may not be prepared. We just do not know when that ending will take place. One day we will all face death.

Our bodies were never made to last forever. As we age, our eyesight grows dim. Our hearing becomes dull. Our joints begin to ache.

The average American male has a life expectancy of 74.4 years. The average American woman lives to be 79.8. Death is the ultimate equalizer. It does not matter if you are rich or poor, famous or unknown, young or old, we all will face death one day. Recently, Skip Prosser, the basketball coach at Wake Forest unexpectedly died of a heart attack at the relatively young age of 56. He was found slumped over in his office. Earlier in the day he had been jogging. My great grandmother lived to be 100. My grandmother lived to be 99. However, to live that long is an exception. Many others have died much younger. All of us will face death.

Now this discussion may seem to be morbid to you, but it is the reality of life. And that brings us to our big question. Is there life after death?

If there is life after death, wouldn't you want to know the answer to that question? Wouldn't you want to experience it or know what to expect?

Sean Penn and Naomi Watts starred in a movie called 21 Grams. The publicity for the movie contains the following quote, *"They say we all lose 21 grams at the exact moment of death...everyone. The weight of a stack of nickels. The weight of a chocolate bar. The weight of a humming bird. Is that all one soul is worth at death---21 grams?"*

We are all familiar with or heard stories about near death experiences where people apparently died and saw themselves hovering above the operating table. Many saw a brilliant white light that they were attracted to and were moving towards. They all suddenly "came back to life" and regained consciousness. Many went on to relay their stories to others. However, did they really die? Did they really come back to life? Was this experience a foreshadowing of things to come?

The ultimate proof of whether or not there is life after death would be if someone who actually died were to come back to life. However, someone did come back from the dead. Of course, that is what the bible says happened to Jesus. Before Houdini, the great magician, died, he said to this wife that after his death he would make every attempt to communicate with the living. However, no one has ever heard from Houdini, but they have heard from Jesus Christ.

You know the story, but let me fill in a few details. On a dark evening in Jerusalem, in the middle of the night, Jesus was betrayed, in a garden, into the hands of the religious and political authorities of his day. He went through the mockery of six trials; three religious and three political. He was eventually condemned to death by the Roman authorities.

He was turned over to the professional Roman executioners. They flogged him with whips that virtually flayed him alive. They beat him and put a crown of thorns on his head. They then nailed him to a cross and left him to die. A Roman centurion eventually certified that he was dead. They thrust a spear into his side to make sure that he was dead. His friends removed him from the cross and buried him in a borrowed grave. For three days, he rested in that grave. The grave was sealed and a guard was assigned to guard the tomb.

However, on the third day, the stone was rolled away. Jesus rose from the dead. He came back to life. His body and soul were reunited. He appeared before Peter and over 500 witnesses. He lived amongst the believers for the next 40 days and nights until he ascended into heaven. He declared victory over death. He proved that there was life after death.

Now you may not believe this account about the resurrection of Jesus. It was taken entirely from the historical writings of the bible. However, if there is a God and if there is life after death, wouldn't it make sense that God would demonstrate that by sending someone to die and come back to life? What greater proof could there be? What if that person, who was sent on this mission, was his only son?

Paul, who was a first century skeptic, eventually came to know Christ personally. He had been a critic and a persecutor of the early church. He claimed to have seen an appearance of the resurrected Christ while traveling on a road to the city of Damascus. He saw a bright light and heard the voice of Jesus speaking to him from the light. He wrote to the church in Corinth that if Jesus was not raised from the dead then believers of all people are most to be pitied. If Jesus was not raised from the dead then their faith was worthless. If Jesus was not raised from the dead then believers are actually false witnesses of the resurrection of Christ.

     However, if Jesus has been raised from the dead then there is life after death. The basic question has been answered. Eternal life is found in a personal relationship with Christ. When you put your personal faith in Christ as your Lord and Savior and turn to him for forgiveness of sins, He will forgive your sins and give you the gift of eternal life. Yes, there is life after death!

To read what the bible says about the resurrection and life after death read 1 Corinthians chapter 15.

Chapter 9

The Big Question
Is there really such a thing as Miracles?

One of my favorite television shows, several years ago, was the X-Files. The punch line was "I want to believe." Of course, the show was all about the search for and existence of alien life and the paranormal. There was a pursuit of something beyond the "normal." That is how I feel about miracles. I want to believe!

What is a miracle? A miracle is something that happens beyond the scope of science and the natural laws. A miracle is something "supernatural" with no scientific explanation. It goes beyond reason and even common sense. It goes beyond science and the natural laws of the universe.

When I refer to miracles, I am not referring in general terms to the "miracle" of a baby being born or the "miracle" of winning the lottery. I am referring to something that happens beyond the realm of normal thinking and possibilities.

Today, miracles have gotten a "bad rap." Maybe because of some televangelists who claim to make the blind to see or the lame to walk? Or maybe it is the "miracle," where one arm is shorter than the other and somehow the arms become equal in length. "Send in your $100 and get your personal miracle."

Do miracles happen today? Maybe the better question is "*Can* miracles happen today?"

First, let us look at some examples of miracles in the Bible. Some have the misconception that there is a miracle on every page. Actually, there were three periods of time in the Bible where the majority of the miracles take place. The three periods were in the days of Moses, the days of Elijah, and the days of Jesus.

In the days of Moses, we see Moses striking the rock resulting in water gushing out of the rock in the desert. A series of miracles take place through Moses when he confronts Pharaoh to let the children of Israel go out of Egypt. When they finally leave, Moses parts the Red Sea to escape the Egyptian army.

In the days of Elijah, we see fire called down

from heaven. We see widow's bowls of flour and jars of oil that are never exhausted. We read of his ascent into heaven on a blazing chariot at the end of his life.

In the days of Jesus, numerous miracles take place and many, but not all, are recorded in the Bible. (Note John 20:30-31) Jesus restores the sight of the man born blind. He heals the lame. He walks on water. He multiplies the fish and loaves. He heals the sick. He turns water into wine. He raises Lazarus from the dead.

Can God do miracles? Part of the answer will depend on your personal view of God. What is your God like? What is his character? What are his attributes? Does he involve himself in the affairs of man?

If you believe that God is the Creator God of the universe, then the possibility of miracles exists. If God is the Creator God, then he created the laws of nature and science. He designed and created what we call "normal." If God is the Creator God and sustainer of all things (see Colossians 1:16-17), then the answer is "yes." Miracles can happen. If you do not believe in a sovereign, Creator God, then you probably will not believe in miracles. Does God do miracles today? I believe he does.

In my opinion, the greatest miracle that has ever happened is the raising of Jesus from the dead. There is no good explanation for what happened to the body of Jesus and the empty tomb. Did the disciples steal the body? Not very likely. Would someone die a martyr's death for what they know to be a lie? Did the Jews steal the body? Impossible. They could have destroyed Christianity "in the womb" by merely placing the body in a cart and walking it through Jerusalem. Did the women go to the wrong tomb? (Pretty demeaning of women, don't you think?) Well, someone had to know where the right tomb was. Maybe Jesus never died on the cross. Somehow, the cold, damp tomb revived Jesus and he pushed aside the two-ton stone, beat up the guard, and declared, "I'm risen from the dead." That takes a tremendous amount of faith to believe. It means the trained Roman executioners made a major mistake. However, no Jews or Disciples or Romans ever doubted the fact that Jesus was dead.

There is no rational explanation for the

empty tomb, except that a miracle took place and that God raised Jesus from the dead. If this is true (and I believe it is), then this means the claims of Jesus were also true. He is the Son of God as he claimed. He did die for our sins on the cross. And that he does offer eternal life and forgiveness of sins, to all who repent and turn to him in faith.

Yes! Miracles happen today. I do believe!

Chapter 10

The Big Question
Was Jesus really Resurrected from the Dead?

What is Easter all about? There are lots of symbols and traditions associated with Easter. The word "easter" does not appear in our bibles, yet it is always associated with Christianity. It is one of the holiest days of the year on the Christian calendar alongside of Christmas. Some would say it surpasses Christmas in its importance. However, the original word has a secular origin and meaning. Here is what some say of the origin of Easter:

"According to the Venerable Bede, Easter derives its name from Eostre, an Anglo-Saxon goddess of spring. A month corresponding to April had been named "Eostremonat," or Eostre's month, leading to "Easter" becoming applied to the Christian holiday that usually took place within it. Prior to that, the holiday had been called Pasch (Passover), which remains its name in most non-

English languages. (Based on the similarity of their names, some connect Eostre with Ishtar, the Babylonian and Assyrian goddess of love and fertility, but there is no solid evidence for this.)

It seems probable that around the second century A.D., Christian missionaries seeking to convert the tribes of northern Europe noticed that the Christian holiday commemorating the resurrection of Jesus roughly coincided with the Teutonic springtime celebrations, which emphasized the triumph of life over death. Christian Easter gradually absorbed the traditional symbols."[9]

What do you think of when you think about Easter? We often think of Easter bunnies and Easter lilies. We think of Easter baskets filled with candy. We think of painting Easter eggs. We think of Easter egg hunts. Or maybe it's an Easter parade down main street. Some of us think of dressing up in our best clothing and going to a crowded church on Easter Sunday morning. (Some of us are like Easter lilies and "bloom once a year.") What do you think about when you think of Easter? For me I think of the early Sunday

---

[9] http://www.factmonster.com/spot/easterintro1.html

morning after the death of Christ.

What does the bible say about the events in the life of Christ leading up to that Sunday morning? The four gospels lay out the details. Each account gives a slightly different snap shot of what took place. (Not contradictory accounts, but complimentary accounts.)

In John 13 we find Jesus in the upper room with the disciples before the Feast of the Passover. Here Jesus washes the feet of the disciples. Here they eat the "last supper." Here Jesus announces his betrayal. The morsel is given to Judas, who leaves the upper room to betray the Son of God. John writes of that moment, *"So after receiving the morsel he (Judas) went out immediately; and it was night."* (John 13:30)

Later that evening Jesus goes to the garden of Gethsemane with his disciples to pray. *"And He came out and proceeded as was His custom to the Mount of Olives; and the disciples also followed Him.* (Matthew 22:39) While there, a crowd of officials and soldiers arrive and Judas betrays Jesus with a kiss. Throughout that night and early morning of the next day, Jesus goes through the mockery of six trials: three political and three religious. He is turned over to the Roman authorities, who mock Him, beat Him, spit on Him, and scourge Him to the point of death. He is literally flayed alive. His flesh separates from organs. A crown of thorns is crushed upon His head. The decision is made by Pilate to crucify Him.

Crucifixion was the chosen method of death for traitors, murderers, and enemies of the Roman state. It was a form of extreme torture and suffering. Often times the victim would live for several days on the cross until exposure and exhaustion led to death.

Jesus is led to the place of crucifixion, to the place of the skull or Golgotha. He is too weak to carry His own cross, so a man, Simon of Cyrene, is forced to carry His cross. *"When they came to the place called The Skull, there they crucified Him and the criminals, one on the right and the other on the left."* (Luke 23:33) *"And above His head they put up the charge against Him which read, "**THIS IS JESUS THE KING OF THE JEWS**."* (Matthew 27:37) *"It was the third hour (9am) when they crucified Him."* (Mark 15:25) *"When the sixth hour (noon) came, darkness fell over the whole land* *until the ninth hour (3pm) At the ninth hour Jesus cried out with a loud voice,* **'ELOI, ELOI, LAMA, SABACHTANI**? *Which is translated,* **'MY GOD, MY GOD, WHY HAVE YOU FORSAKEN ME?'"** (Mark 15:33-34) At that point the sins of the entire world are placed upon Jesus. All the sins that have ever been sinned or ever will be sinned. That means all sins; past, present, and future. Jesus died for them all. *"Therefore, when Jesus had received the sour wine (on the cross), He said, 'It is finished!' And He bowed His head and gave up His Spirit."* (John 19:30)

Because the Passover would begin at dusk, the Jewish authorities wanted the bodies off of the crosses. *"Then the Jews, because if was the day of preparation, so that the bodies would not remain on the cross on the Sabbath (for that Sabbath was a high day), asked Pilate that their legs might be broken (to hasten their death), and that they might be taken away."* (John 19:31) The soldiers break the legs of the two on the crosses besides Jesus. But when they came to Jesus, they did not break His legs. They thrust a spear in His side. Immediately, blood and water rushed out of the wound. Jesus was declared dead by the

Roman executioners.

The body is laid in a borrowed tomb. Jesus is laid to rest. A large stone is rolled across the opening to the tomb. A Roman seal is attached to the stone. A guard is placed before the tomb to guard the body from the disciples or anyone else. But then Sunday comes! *"Now on the first day of the week Mary Magdalene came early to the tomb, while it was still dark, and saw the stone already taken away from the tomb."* (John 20:1) An angel appears to Mary Magdalene and the other Mary and says, *"Do not be afraid; for I know that you are looking for Jesus who has been crucified. He is not here, for He has risen, just as He said. Come, see the place where He was lying."* (Matthew 28:5-6)

On Easter Sunday, the Sunday after the crucifixion of Jesus, the tomb is found empty! What happened to the body of Jesus? Lots of theories abound to explain away the resurrection of Christ.

One theory is that the women went to the wrong tomb. If the women went to the wrong tomb, then all the authorities had to do was to go to the right tomb. They could have gotten the body of Jesus placed it in a cart and wheeled it through the streets of Jerusalem. Christianity would have "died in the womb." Another theory is that Jesus didn't die on the cross. When He was placed in the tomb, the cold, damp tomb awakened Him. But that means the trained Roman executioners were wrong. That means that Jesus was able to push aside the two-ton stone, break through the seal, fight and defeat the Roman guard and declare to His disciples, "I am risen from the dead." A very unlikely theory.

Another theory is that the disciples stole the body. The "meek and mild disciples," who had deserted Christ, beat the Roman guards, rolled away the stone, broke the Roman seal, and were willing to die torturous deaths for something that they knew was a lie. Not possible. You might die for something that you knew to be true, but it would be unthinkable to die for something that you knew to be a lie. But this was the explanation concocted by the Jewish religious leaders to explain away the empty tomb. (Matthew 28:11-13)

So why was the tomb empty on Easter Sunday? Because Jesus had come back to life. He had risen. He had been resurrected from the dead. And that my friends is the true meaning of Easter, Jesus Christ has died for my sins, your sins, and the sins of the whole world, and has risen from the dead.

In 1 Corinthians 15 we read Paul's classic treatise on the resurrection of Christ. He declares that the death, burial, and resurrection of Christ is of first importance. He states that the resurrected Christ has appeared alive to Peter, to the Apostles, to 500 of the brethren, and to him. He states that if the resurrection of Christ did not happen, then the following would be true of believers. Our faith is vain. Our faith is worthless. We have been found to be false witnesses of the resurrection. Those who have died in Christ have perished. We are of all men most to be pitied.

"But now Christ has been raised from the dead, the first fruits of those who are asleep." (1 Corinthians 15:20) If Jesus Christ has been raised from the dead, then Easter Sunday is the most important day of the year. It is the day we celebrate His resurrection from the dead. We celebrate forgiveness of our sins. We celebrate a new life. We have a hope for the future. We have

heaven and eternity awaiting us. The sting of death has been removed. The penalty for our sins has been paid.

My friend if you have never trusted Christ as your Savior, what better day than Easter Sunday to put your faith in Him.

"But thanks be to God, who gives us the victory through our Lord Jesus Christ! Therefore, my beloved brethren, be steadfast, immovable, always abounding in the work of the Lord, knowing that your toil is not in vain in the Lord." (1 Corinthians 15:57-58)

Discussion Questions:
1. What are some of your Easter traditions?
2. Why is the resurrection of Jesus Christ so important?
3. If Jesus was not raised from the dead, then what does that say about our faith? What does it say about our eternal security?
4. Why do so many people today deny the resurrection and believe the various wrong theories about the empty tomb?
5. What is the best way to prepare your heart for Easter?

Chapter 11

The Big Question
What about all the other Religions?

This big question can be answered by the response to another question, "Is Jesus the only way to god?" You may want to read the article that addresses that question. But here, I want to address this question a little more directly.

If Jesus is the only way to God, then all other religions are excluded. Obviously, this raises an immediate storm of protest. How can you Christians be so narrow minded and intolerant of other views? Are you really saying that that no other religion can get you to God? This seems mighty unfair. Let's address that question.

But we are getting ahead of ourselves, so let me first digress. First let me define a couple of terms. What is religion? Religion is man's best attempt to reach God. It is a system of beliefs, practices, and traditions. Usually there is a sacred writing accompanying religion, like the Bible, the book of Koran, or the Bahagavita. Also, there is usually a founder of the religion or primary proponent.

How do you define God? The Greek word for God is theos. It is the root word for our English word "theology," which is the study of God. God is the supreme being of the universe. God is outside the bounds of the finite. There are several different ways that people think about God. Let me generalize and give you four major categories.

Someone who believes in God is a theist. The Latin word for God is deo. Someone who believes in God is a "deist." Most of the founding fathers of America claimed to be deists, believers in God. Many held a foundational belief in God. However, they had differing views on what that god was like.

There are four main views regarding the existence of God. A theist believes in the existence of God. More on that later. An agnostic is not sure if there is a god. The word "agnostic" comes from two Greek words. The prefix "a" means "not" or "no." The word "gnostic" means knowledge. The agnostic is saying that God is outside of his knowledge. There may or may not be a god. He simply is not sure if there is a god. Many people fall into this category.

The atheist is in a completely different category. The word has the prefix "a" in front of the word for God. The atheist says there is no god. They categorically reject the notion that there is a god. God cannot and does not exist. They deny the possibility of the existence of God.

In my experience I've met many agnostics, but few that are truly atheists. I'm sure in other parts of the world that experience would be quite different. However, I have met many people who are "practical atheist." These are people who claim to believe in God, but live as though God does not exist.

Now let me return to theism. Theism can be put into several different broad categories. The mono-theist believes in one God. This is the primary Judeo-Christian view. There is one God. This view is also true of the religion of Islam. It is interesting that all three of these religions have their origin in the same geographical context.

The second view is pantheism. This view says that God is in everything and is everything. The prefix "pan" means "all." God is in the rocks, trees, sky, animals, etc. God is everywhere. God is everything.

The view of poly theism says that there are many gods, not just one. There are multiple gods to believe in. It reminds me of the Greek and Roman gods. Gods of war. Gods of love. Gods of thunder, etc. There was a god for almost everything and for every occasion.

The final view about God that I would like to suggest is secular humanism. It's really not a form of theism, but to me it is a form of religion, although I may get some dispute here. It has its own belief system. It requires "faith." There is something you must believe. In simple terms secular humanism is a religion with man as its god and at its center. If humankind continues to grow, develop, and progress, then the world will become a better and better place. This view is based on improving and self-effort. It has a very optimistic view of the potential of improvement of mankind. This view is independent of God. It would like to remove God from the equation.

As you can see from this brief discussion on religion, there are many forms of religion. I've only just touched the very tip of the iceberg. Each of these forms of religion has its own system of beliefs.

To simplify matters, I would like to categorize all religions into three very general and broad groups. The first group is performance-based religion.

Performance based religion says that you must do something to earn approval from God. You must strictly adhere to a strict code of conduct or else face the disapproval of God. In this system you must <u>do</u> something for approval. The problem with this view is how do you know if you have ever done enough? How will you ever know if your good deeds out-weigh your bad deeds?

The second broad category is based on who you are as a person. You must be a certain person to earn god's approval. God loves you if you are kind, loving, generous, or inclusive. In this system you must <u>be</u> something in order to gain god's approval. The problem is how can you become more kind, loving, generous, and inclusive? How good is good enough? It is interesting to read what the New Testament says about this problem. Matthew 5:48 states, *"Therefore you are to be perfect, as your heavenly father is perfect."* Matthew seems to be saying that the standard is perfection. Has anyone anywhere reached perfection? James says in James 2:10, *"For whoever keeps the whole law and yet stumbles in one point, he has become guilty of all."* In other words, if you lived in total obedience to god's laws your whole life and then on your death bed sinned, you would be guilty of breaking all the laws. By the way, when Moses threw down the tablets that had the ten commandments written on them, how many laws did he break?

    The last general category is the grace-based model of religion. This model suggests that approval from God cannot be earned. This is the Christian view of religion. It does not matter how kind, loving, generous, or inclusive you may be. This view says that salvation is a gift that can only be received. It is impossible to earn your way to god's approval. You can never become "good enough" on your own effort. Read what Titus says in Titus 3:5, *"He saved us, not on the basis of deeds which we have done..."* Paul says in Ephesians 2:8-9, *"For by grace you have been saved through faith; and that not of yourselves, it is the gift of god; not as a result of works, so that no one may boast."*

Our good deeds will never outweigh our bad deeds. We will never completely obey the "golden rule." We can never change ourselves enough to earn approval from God.

This view says that God alone can save us from our sins. Salvation from sin is what gives us approval with God. Salvation is a gift from God that is freely given and must be freely received with "no strings" attached.

Obviously, this is the Christian view of salvation. The bible makes clear that Jesus is the one who died for the sins of the world. Probably the most famous verse in the bible is John 3:16. You can see that verse on placards at football games. "For god so loved the world, that he gave his only begotten son, that whoever believes in him shall not perish, but have eternal life."

So, what about all the other religions? In my life I have put my faith in Jesus Christ as my personal savior and lord. As a sophomore at the University of Maryland, I came to know Christ on a personal basis. Since then, my life has never been the same.

Chapter 12

The Big Question
What about Women?

On our planet, there are many more women than men. According to the 2008 U.N. Statistics Division, there are 3,442,850,573 women and 3,386,509,865 men. In other words, there are 1.016638 women per man on the earth. Most of our churches and civic organizations are also filled with women. Some would say they do 90% of the work of those organizations, which is probably a little low.

The modern feminism movement was an outcry against how women have been treated in our society. After all, women did not get the right to vote until August 18, 1920 with the passing of the 19th Amendment to the US Constitution. This right came as a direct result of the women's suffrage (the right to vote) movement in the mid 1800's and early 1900's. Thank God, there were women who stood up for their rights.

Some religions limit women in their worship

of God. In the places of worship of some religions, the women are not allowed to worship with the men. There are fences that separate the men and women. They gather in separate courtyards. In some cultures, women are held in very low esteem.

In the Roman culture of the first century, women had very few rights and privileges. A man's wife was his property. A man could be involved in multiple affairs, but a woman could do nothing about it. If she was caught in an affair, she could be put to death without a trial. Marriages were arranged. Families gave their daughters away in marriage, but they had to carry with them a certain price. Without a proper dowry, forget the marriage.

Since the beginning of time there have been women on this planet. Women have had our babies and raised our children. Women have kept our homes. Women have educated our children. Women have been leaders in society. Women have served on the Supreme Court. Women have become famous authors, poets, and philosophers. Women have been leading scientists. Women have flown into space. Women are presidents of companies. Women serve on the boards of insurance companies. There is nothing that a woman can't do. A woman will one day be President of the United States. So, what is the big deal about women?

First of all, thank God for women. And thank God specifically for my wife. My wife has done an excellent job raising and educating our children. She has kept our home together. She has been a leader in our community. She helped to found a Christian school. She has traveled to China and abroad. She has been my lover and best friend for 40 years. I thank God for my wife. I thank God for women.

The creation story says that Eve was taken from the rib of Adam. From that rib God fashioned a woman—a beautiful, eye-popping woman. The first woman on the earth and Adam was completely startled and surprised. He was flabbergasted. His life was turned completely upside down. Nothing was ever the same. He was stunned by her. (And men are still stunned today.) Note she was taken from the rib. The ribs are what protects the heart. The ribs safely keep all the other internal organs in place. Without ribs we would be like a bowl of jelly. But the ribs, mostly guard the heart. The heart is what pumps blood through our system and keeps us alive. Metaphorically, the heart is the seat of our emotions.

Isn't it interesting that Eve was made from the side of Adam—not from the feet, hands, or head? Adam and Eve were created to complement each other. They were meant to be companions. They were meant to be friends. They were meant to be lovers.

They were created equal. They were created equal in every way. Equal in value, importance, and significance. Equal partners in life.

The woman was also created to be superior to man. The woman is infinitely superior to a man at being a woman. She has a unique view on life. She often feels more deeply than men. She often is more tender, kind, and caring. She often is more intuitive and discerning. She also can be stronger in many ways.

Women are mysterious to men. I know, because I am married to one. Often men can barely understand their thinking and emotions.

Men (and I am one of them) have difficulty understanding how women process information. Women can talk through issues. I heard an estimate that women speak about 20,000 words per day. A man speaks about 500 words per day. This statistic alone explains a major difference in how men and women communicate. Why is this so? I think it is because of God's unique design of women.

The body of a woman is obviously much different than the body of a man. Women you drive us men crazy. And most of you know it. It's amazing what a flutter of an eye or the movement of a hip or the show of an ankle can do to a man. Why do you think advertisers use gorgeous, beautiful women to sell us soap, detergent, and Hardee's hamburgers?

What is the role of women in the church? What should be her role? I want to look at a couple of passages from the Bible that gives us some insight on the subject.

"Let women keep silent in the church and receive instructions at home." (1 Corinthians 14:34)

What could this possibly mean?

Understanding the culture of the day may help. In the Jewish culture of First Century Israel, when this was written, things were very different than the culture of today. At least generally in the USA we find things different. In the culture of the First Century women worshiped separately from men. There was absolutely no female leadership role in the synagogue. The women were truly silent. But after the New Testament church was born at Pentecost, the role of women changed dramatically.

     Women in the church had a new found freedom to worship. Men and women worshiped God together. They took Communion together. They prayed together. The broke bread together. Numerous women are mentioned in the gospels. One group of women supported Jesus and the Apostles through their private means. (The first missionary support team were all women. Check out Luke 8:3-4). The story of the women at the well is an excellent example of how Jesus broke down the barriers of race, religion, nationality, custom, and gender. (John 4) After the resurrection, the first-person Jesus spoke to was a woman. (John 20:15)

In the book of Acts, we learn of Lydia. Lydia was a wealthy business woman. She became the first convert in Europe. We hear of Damaris coming to know Jesus. She was part of the Areopagus in Athens. (Acts 17) We read of Priscilla, wife of Aquila from Italy. In 2 Timothy we are reminded of the faith of Lois that was passed onto her daughter, Eunice, who passed on that same faith to Timothy. The list goes on and on of important, valued, gifted women in the New Testament.

In Colossians women continue to play a prominent role. Nymphas and the church in her home is mentioned.

Maybe the women in this church were exercising their new found freedom a little much and had to be instructed to be quiet and ask their questions at home to their husbands. I'm not sure what the issue was that prompted this passage.

It is interesting that the word for deacon is mentioned in relation to a woman in Romans 16:1. "*I commend to you our sister Phoebe, who is a servant of the church which is at Cenchrea.*" This was leaving the door open for female deacons. (Some Pastors are having a coronary right now.) How about women elders?   Not really sure. Certainly, in all the verses referring to elders it refers to men. But how about the unnamed woman mentioned in 2 John 1 and 2? *"The elder to the chosen lady and her children, whom I love in truth."* How about women pastors? Not really sure again, but again all the examples and reference seem to point towards men. Why am I choosing to stir up these questions?

     Let me summarize with this. What about women? Women are God's chosen creation. Women are equal with men in value, significance, and important. Women have all the rights to worship and prayer as men. The bottom line is that Christianity, more than any other religion, raises women up and liberates them. Christianity sets women free. Sets them free to be all that God wants them to be.

     Thank God for women!

This article was written by Earle J. Chute with a lot of consultation with women including my own wife.

Chapter 13

The Big Question
What happened to the Dinosaurs?

There are several ways to answer this question. One is scientific, one is philosophic, and the other is religious. My greater expertise is in the religious realm, although I majored in biology in college. But I will give some attempt to give an answer in all three fields.

Dinosaurs are "terrible lizards." In my child hood I remember watching the television cartoon, the Flintstones. I laughed with many others while watching the lives of Fred, Wilma, and Barney. The dinosaurs were everything but terrible lizards. My next image of the dinosaurs came from the Steven Spielberg movies beginning with Jurassic Park. In both of those examples the dinosaurs roamed freely with humans. However, all archeologists believe that in actuality the major dinosaurs, like T Rex, Stegosaurus, Brontosaurus, etc. lived millions of years before humans were ever on the planet. Did the dinosaurs and humans live together at the same time? What happened to those dinosaurs?

Often this question is posed with certain presuppositions in mind. Namely, how could a credible person actually believe the bible record, especially the creation story and a young earth. It would seem that a Christian would have to put their brain on the shelf in order to believe the bible. I really do not think that that has to be the case. You can be an anthropologist or an archeologist or a scientist and believe the bible.

Here some possible scientific explanations of what happened to the dinosaurs.
1) They all went extinct for a variety of reasons according to the principles of Darwinian evolution.
2) They all died because of world-wide climatic temperature change caused by a cloud formed by a large comet or meteor impact that blocked the sun and produced global cooling. (Temperatures much too cold for cold blooded reptiles to survive.)
3) Dinosaurs were all killed by a worldwide flood and/or did not survive the post flood world.

Philosophically, we may argue that the

dinosaurs went the way of all animals, reptiles, plants, etc that did not survive natural selection and did not evolve to survive in the changing world conditions. It was inevitable and natural that they all died. Their time on earth was over.

Now here is a possible biblical explanation. Let me begin by saying that I believe in a literal interpretation of the bible. Of course, I leave room for figures of speech, metaphors, parables, and hyperboles. But none the less, I take a literal view of the scriptures.

The world was covered by a water vapor canopy before a worldwide flood. (In our solar system often, there is a gas canopy of the most common elements on the surface of the planet, in our case the oceans water.) This water vapor created higher temperatures, more moisture, and better conditions for cold blooded reptiles to survive. There were tropical, jungle like conditions around the globe. This may explain why tropical plants have been found on the frozen poles and on the tops of mountains.

Then a worldwide flood occurred, that covered the surface of the earth with water. This would obviously kill all breathing land animals, reptiles, etc. Noah would have taken two of each species onto the ark. (Obviously, the dinosaurs did not have to be full grown on entering the ark. They could have been at an early life size, like the size of a sheep.) After the flood, all the animals left the ark. However, the climate had changed dramatically. The dinosaurs did not survive the climatic changes that they faced.

Which of the above arguments require faith? Which requires the most faith? My contention is that all of the above arguments require faith. It requires just as much faith to believe in Darwinian evolution as it does to believe in the six-day creation story.

What happened to the dinosaurs? They all died. (Although, there still remains today the occasional "pre-historic, extinct fish" that shows up in a fisherman's net. It does make you wonder what unknown creatures still live beneath the deep seas of the earth. And what about the alligators, crocs, and other reptiles that are virtually no different than their pre-historic cousins?)

Chapter 14

The Big Question
What is a REAL man?

Today in our society there is a great lack of "real" men. Where are all the men today? They are not in the churches. They are not in ministries outside the church. They are bailing out of marriages. They are absent as fathers. The divorce rates are not much different inside and outside the church. What happened to all the "real" men?

The media today often portrays men as lazy, stupid, out of touch, imbeciles. (Every now and then there is a Jack Bauer in 24 or Aragon in the Lord of the Rings! However, they are exceptions.) Look at the cartoons in the newspapers. What are the popular shows on television? How are men portrayed on those shows?

The bible says a lot about the role of men in society. Men are to be the heads of the home. Men are to be leaders in the church. Men are the leaders in the community. (Of course, women also play important, vital roles in all those areas I just mentioned, but that is not the topic of discussion here.) Men are fathers to their children. They are to be protectors and providers for their families. They are to be mentors and examples to their sons. Today there is a great lacking of older men who serve in those roles. There are very few positive examples. What happened to all the "real" men?

     I would suggest that there have been three strong negative influences on men. The first, the pursuit of <u>pleasure</u>. The web has opened the door to pornography. More men are hooked on porn than ever before in our history. It is easily accessible with the click of a mouse. No sneaking in the door with an adult magazine in a paper bag. You can bring it into the privacy of your home. This has destroyed the souls of men. Men are looking at images that are permanently etched in their thoughts. What woman can compare to those airbrushed images? It creates a longing that can never be righteously satisfied. I believe this has made men passive, guilt ridden, and sexually promiscuous. It has been devastating. It has destroyed countless marriages and families.

A second negative influence has been the search for <u>possessions</u>. Men are not easily satisfied. We want the most recent things and we want it now. We want the latest and the best. We want to have what our parents have only we want it now. We are willing to work 80 hour weeks to achieve those possessions. We are willing to sacrifice all for the material things. We are willing to sacrifice our wives, children, friends, and even our health.

The third negative influence is the desire for <u>power</u>. Power over people. Power over our future. Power over our circumstances. We want to be in a position where we are never obligated to others. Where we are never dependent on others. (Not sure how this fits in with our entitlement society.) Power is a reflection of ego. We want to be the center of our own universe. We want to be the king. We want to be in charge. It is placing ourselves on the throne of our lives.

Those three negative influences (and we could name many others) have destroyed the heart, soul, and spirit of men. What is the solution?

I would like to talk about what it means to

be a "real" man. Not a perfect man, a "real" man. I will be sharing from the scriptures what it means to be a "real" man. Lots of my thoughts come from my good friend and mentor, David English, who has written extensively on this topic. Also, some of these ideas originated with Robert Lewis of Fellowship Bible Church, who wrote the book, Raising a Modern Day Knight.

Here are some words that describe a "real" man:

Godly	Leader	Tough	Disciplined
Courageous	Integrity	Tender	Sensitive
Keeps word	Respectful	Kind	Compassionate
Servant	Righteous	Holy	Discerning
Protector	Provider	Pure	Generous
Sacrificial	Initiator	Brave	Humility
Assertive	Worshipper	Loving	Righteous

You may want to circle those words that are true of your life. It is a good way to measure how you are doing as a "real" man.

There are four pillars of a "real" man. A "real" man rejects passivity. A "real" man expects God's greater reward. A "real" man accepts responsibility. A "real" man leads courageously. I would like to explain each of these pillars and then illustrate it with an example from the Bible.

Pillar One: Rejects Passivity

What this means is that a "real" man takes charge of his own life. He is not passive. He takes the initiative. He pro-actively seeks to obey the scriptures. He loves his wife. He leads his family. He protects and provides for his family. He sacrifices his own desires because of his love for Christ. He is willing to put others first. He is a servant.

Nehemiah was an example of this in the Old Testament. In Nehemiah 1:1-2:5 we see how Nehemiah rejected passivity. He had heard how the walls of Jerusalem had been destroyed and was granted permission by a heathen King to return to Jerusalem. On arrival he saw the condition of the walls of Jerusalem. The walls had been broken down. He didn't accept their condition. He set his mind like flint to accomplish the task of rebuilding in the face of adversaries. In 52 days the work was accomplished and the walls were rebuilt to the glory of God.

I love the scene from the Lord of the Rings at the council of Elrond at Rivendell. The people of Middle Earth are discussing what to do with the ring of power and how to destroy it. The small voice of Frodo Baggins speaks out, "I'll take the ring to Mordor, but I don't know the way." Frodo rejects passivity and is willing to take on the responsibility of destroying the ring, although he has very little idea what that would entail.

Pillar Two: Expects God's Greater Reward

A "real" man is expecting for his reward to be given in heaven. He wants to hear the words of his Master, "Well done, my good and faithful servant." He lives by the words of Paul, "Moreover, it is required of stewards that they be found faithful." He realizes that on earth he may not receive his full reward, because something greater is awaiting him. He is living with an eternal perspective. He is majoring on those things that are really important in life.

Paul was an example of this in the New

Testament. In Paul's last letter before his death, he writes in 2 Timothy 4:6-8, *"For I am already being poured out as a drink offering, and the time of my departure has come. I have fought the good fight, I have finished the race, I have kept the faith. Henceforth there is laid up for me the crown of righteousness, which the Lord, the righteous judge, will award to me on that Day, and not only to me but also to all who have loved his appearing."* Nothing could take away his reward. He came close to death on numerous occasions because he expected God's greater reward. This expectation made him boldly courageous and fearless.

Jim Elliot, who gave his life in missionary service to the Auca Indians of Ecuador, said before his death, "He is no fool who gives what he cannot keep to gain that which he cannot lose." He is already enjoying his greater reward!

Pillar Three: Accepts Responsibility

A "real" man accepts the responsibilities that the Lord has given him. If he is a husband, then he is to love his wife as Christ loves the

Church. If he is a father, he is to provide for and protect his children. He is to be a mentor and example to them. He is to live out the Spirit-filled life at home, at work, and at play. He accepts his God given role as the head of his home. He does not shirk his responsibilities out of fear or a sense of inadequacy. He trusts the Lord to live out his faith on a daily basis.

Barnabas in the New Testament was an example of this quality. He was constantly accepting responsibility for those around him. He sells his own possessions and gives the proceeds to the church. He takes the new believer Saul under his wing and helps him in his initial growth. He defends his cousin John Mark, even though it results in a split with Paul. He was always accepting responsibility.

In the movie, <u>Saving Private Ryan</u>. Paratrooper, private James Francis Ryan (Matt Damon) is the last-surviving brother of four servicemen. The other three were killed during the earlier stages of the war. U.S. Army Captain John H. Miller (Tom Hanks) is commanded to find and save Private Ryan, so he can return to home. Miller accepts that responsibility along with seven other men. They risk their own lives to rescue Private Ryan. Some give up their lives in battle, but Private Ryan is found and brought back home. Like a good commanding officer we need to learn to accept responsibility.

Pillar Four: Leads Courageously

A "real" man is willing to lay his life on the line. It takes courage to be a leader. A leader has to overcome his own fears and step forward to lead. A leader has followers. A leader is an example. A leader walks by faith and not by sight. A leader steps into the unknown with a strong confidence in God. He walks through the night holding upright the light of the gospel of the glory of God. He is ready and willing to charge the gates of hell.

I think of the great leaders of the Civil War. One of my favorites is Col. Joshua Lawrence Chamberlain. He was the commander of the 20th Maine regiment. He was in command on Little Round Top during the second day of the battle of Gettysburg on July 2, 1863. His command was protecting the extreme left flank of the Union army. During the battle they were in danger of being overrun. Out of ammunition, he makes the bold decision to fix bayonets and charge the Confederate forces down and off of Little Round Top. He leads the charge. He leads his men to victory. The outcome to the battle of Gettysburg is sealed. He was a leader of men (and a very devote believer.) He was awarded the Medal of Honor for his gallantry at Gettysburg.

    Joshua is an example of leadership in the Old Testament. He takes over for Moses and leads Israel into the promised land. He is the commanding general who fights against the enemies of Jehovah. Read about Joshua in Joshua 1:1-9:

"After the death of Moses, the servant of the LORD, the LORD said to Joshua the son of Nun, Moses' assistant, "Moses my servant is dead. Now therefore arise, go over this Jordan, you and all this people, into the land that I am giving to them, to the people of Israel. Every place that the sole of your foot will tread upon I have given to you, just as I promised to Moses. From the wilderness and this Lebanon as far as the great river, the river Euphrates, all the land of the Hittites to the Great

Sea toward the going down of the sun shall be your territory. No man shall be able to stand before you all the days of your life. Just as I was with Moses, so I will be with you. I will not leave you or forsake you. Be strong and courageous, for you shall cause this people to inherit the land that I swore to their fathers to give them. Only be strong and very courageous, being careful to do according to all the law that Moses my servant commanded you. Do not turn from it to the right hand or to the left, that you may have good success wherever you go. This Book of the Law shall not depart from your mouth, but you shall meditate on it day and night, so that you may be careful to do according to all that is written in it. For then you will make your way prosperous, and then you will have good success. Have I not commanded you? Be strong and courageous. Do not be frightened, and do not be dismayed, for the L<small>ORD</small> *your God is with you wherever you go."*

Four things are true of a godly leader. The godly leader embraces the **L**ordship of Christ in his life. The godly leader leads with **e**nthusiasm. The godly leader leads by his **a**ctions. The godly leader leads with **d**etermination. A godly leader---LEADS!

The four pillars of a "real" man are built on a foundation, the chief cornerstone is Jesus Christ. The first step on becoming a "real" man is to put your faith in Jesus Christ. He is the perfect example of a "real" man. He lived out all four of the pillars. He will be the cornerstone of your life. When you receive Jesus Christ as your Savior and become a Christ follower, you will live the life of a "real" man. It is a great adventure!

Discussion Questions for the Four Pillars of a REAL man:

Reject Passivity
1. Why are men so passive?
2. Why are so few men involved in our ministries?
3. Why are so many more women in our ministries?
4. What does it mean to reject passivity?

Expect God's Greater Reward
1. What rewards await believers who walk with God?

2. What can take away your reward?
3. What affect should the expectation of reward have on your daily life?
4. What are the eternal benefits of our reward?

Accept Responsibility
1. What are some of the responsibilities that men must accept?
2. What happens when men don't accept those responsibilities?
3. What does it mean "to take charge" of your own life?
4. What barriers prevent men from accepting responsibility?

Lead Courageously
1. Where are the male leaders?
2. Why does it take courage to lead?
3. What does it mean to lead spiritually?
4. How is spiritual leadership different than the world's model of leadership?

Chapter 15

The Big Question
What is the Gift of Singleness?

In 1 Corinthians 7:7-8 Paul says, *"However, each man has his own gift from God, one in this manner, and another in that. But I say to the unmarried and to widows that it is good for them if they remain even as I."*

Paul seems to be describing singleness as a gift. What does he mean by that statement? Is Paul opposed to marriage? This essay will attempt to answer these questions.

The word "gift" in this passage is the Greek word, charisma. It means a gift of grace. It is freely given. The root word, charis, is often translated grace or kindness. Grace is often defined as God's unmerited, freely bestowed favor. Is singleness God's freely bestowed favor for our lives?

Yes! Paul seems to be saying that singleness is a free gift of God's grace, favor, and kindness. Singleness may be a season before marriage or it may be true of our entire lives. It is a gift.

He goes on to say in verse 8 that this gift is "good." This makes sense, because all of the gifts of God's grace are good. He never gives us a gift that is "bad."

Why would Paul describe singleness as a gift?

First, I would like to digress and talk about the purpose and plan of marriage in God's economy. The purpose of marriage is not just so we can end our "condition" of singleness. It is not just so we can engage in sex with our spouse. It is not just so we can become "complete." I think there is a deeper and more fundamental purpose for marriage.

The ultimate purpose of marriage is to bring greater glory to God. A marriage is a reflection of God's love for the church through Jesus Christ.

In the familiar passage in Ephesians 5:25 Paul says, "Husbands, love your wives, just as Christ also loved the church and gave Himself up for her." How did Christ love the church? How was love demonstrated? He gave Himself up for the church. He gave Himself up as a substitutionary atonement for our sins. He stepped down from heaven and gave His very life for the church. A marriage should reflect that same kind of commitment. True love is not a feeling or emotion. Love is an action verb. Love is a commitment. True love is not dependent upon feelings.

In this passage Paul admonishes the husband three times to love his wife. (vv 25, 28, 33) Why the repetition? Maybe because us men are hard-headed and need to be reminded. Saying "I love you" one time at the altar is not enough. Or maybe Paul is making the strong point that sacrificial love needs to be at the very center of our marriage and that the husband needs to lead in love.

When a marriage is filled with sacrificial love, it will bring glory to God and mutual satisfaction in the marriage.

A marriage is also the result of a covenant. A covenant in the bible is a binding, unconditional commitment between two parties. When a man and woman are standing at the front of the church exchanging their vows, they are sealing a covenant. They are making a binding, unconditional commitment to each other, before God, before each other, before their friends, and before the heavenly host.

Another primary purpose for marriage is the Spiritual and personal growth of the husband and wife. The process of sanctification is intensified and accelerated through marriage. Marriage has an interesting way of revealing our deep-seated selfishness and rebellion. This revealing process is both painful and helpful. It brings to light who we really are as a person. The husband and wife are "naked and not ashamed" physically, emotionally, and spiritually. They will see each other and themselves like they have never seen before.

So, if marriage is so glorious and helpful for our growth, then why is singleness a gift? In the same chapter of Corinthians Paul says in verses 32-35, *"But I want you to be free from concern. One who is unmarried is concerned about the things of the Lord, how he may please the Lord; but one who is married is concerned about the things of the world, how he may please his wife, and his interests are divided. The woman who is unmarried, and the virgin, is concerned about the things of the Lord, that she may be holy both in body and spirit; but one who is married is concerned about the things of the world, how she may please her husband. This I say for your own benefit; not to put a restraint upon you, but to promote what is appropriate and to secure undistracted devotion to the Lord."*

Paul seems to be saying three things:
1) The unmarried is concerned about the things of the Lord.
2) The married has divided interests and time.
3) The unmarried has the opportunity to secure undistracted devotion of the Lord. (Emphasis on "undistracted." Both marrieds and singles should be equally devoted to the Lord.)

Singleness is a gift because it allows you to fix your attention fully upon the Lord. A married person has both "divided" and "distracted" interests.

The word "divided" in verse 34 is merizo. It comes from the word meros, which means to receive one's portion, a part, or a share. A divided person is pushed and challenged in lots of different directions. He has obligations to his wife and children. He must love his family. He must provide for his family. He must lead his family. All of this takes time, energy, and purposefulness.

The word "undistracted" in verse 35 is aperispastos. It begins with the negative prefix a and adds the word perispao. This word means to draw away. The word therefore means not to be drawn away from. The person with the gift of singleness will not be drawn away from their singular devotion to the Lord.

Paul is in no way disparaging marriage. He is merely pointing out the reality that every married person experiences. They are often divided and distracted in their devotion to the Lord.

Please note that I am not saying that singleness is a gift of the Holy Spirit like other charismatic gifts. I am also not saying that singleness is superior to marriage. And I am not saying that a single person should remain single the rest of their lives. Singleness may simply be a season, a very important season of undivided, undistracted devotion to the Lord.

So, what is the best way to get the most out of the gift of singleness? Here are a few words of encouragement and exhortation.

1) I would encourage the single person to do all that they can to grow in their devotion to Christ. Use the extra time and energy to seek the Lord fully and diligently. Be a strong student of the Word of God. Become a powerful person of prayer.

2) I would encourage the single person to find a community of believers that they can fully engage themselves in. (A mixed group of men and women in the same season of life would be very helpful.) Seek to build up and disciple others. Seek to be part of helping to fulfill the great commission.

3) I would exhort the single person to build meaningful friendships with the opposite sex. Seek to grow in your communication skills. Pursue friendship and not a relationship.

4) I would encourage the single person to serve the local community that you live and work in. This may be through your local church or local ministry. It may be through serving the local Salvation Army or soup kitchen. It may be with

other groups that serve the local community. Be actively engaged in serving and loving others, it will get your eyes off of yourself.

Timothy Keller includes a chapter on singleness in his book, The Meaning of Marriage. I highly recommend it and in particular that chapter. Some of my thoughts and ideas for this essay were triggered by his book.

He says, "In his writings, Paul always uses the word "gift" to mean an ability God gives to build others up. Paul is not speaking, then, of some kind of elusive, stress-free state. The 'gift-ness' of being single for Paul lay in the freedom it gave him to concentrate on ministry in ways that a married man could not."[10]

Singleness is truly a gift. It allows you to pursue the Lord with undivided and undistracted devotion. It grants you the freedom and energy to serve the church and the local community. It gives you the opportunity to fully engage in helping to build disciples and fulfill the great commission. Singleness is a gift from God.

---

[10] Timothy Keller, *The Meaning of Marriage*, (New York, New York: Dutton, 2011), pages 207-208.

Chapter 16

The Big Question
What is the Meaning and Purpose of Life?

Let us begin with a quote by the famous philosopher, Lucy when she says to Charlie Brown, "this time I'll let you kick the football." And of course, she doesn't and he misses the football for the hundredth time. How often have you missed the football? Have you really connected your life and work with a purpose and meaning?

In the book by Howard Behar entitled, *It's Not About The Coffee*, he includes the following poem in his introduction:

The work of the world is common as mud,
Botched, it smears the hands, crumbles to dust.
But the thing worth doing well done
has a shape that satisfies, clean, and evident.
Greek amphoras for wine or oil,
Hopi vases that held corn, are put in museums

> *But you know they were made to be used.*
> *The pitcher cries for water to carry*
> *And a person for work that is real.*

---from Marge Piercy's *"To Be of Use"* [11]

    Everything has been made for a purpose. Things are worth doing well. Work is to benefit others. We are searching for meaning and purpose in what we do.

    Throughout all of recorded history there has been a massive search for the lost pirate treasure of Captain Kidd, for the land of El Dorado, for the Fountain of Youth, for Solomon's tomb, and for the Ark of the Covenant. But the greatest search in all of history has been the search for the meaning and purpose of life.

    Why is this search for meaning so important and all so consuming? The answer to that question is the subject of this essay.

    Most people spend one third of their lives working, one third of their lives sleeping, and one third of their lives recreating and all the rest.

---

[11] Howard Behar, *It's Not About the Coffee,* (New York: Penguin Group, 2007), Page x

Imagine that! If you live to be 90 years old, you would have spent 30 years in bed. (No wonder a good mattress and pillow is so important!)

My observation is that people are seeking meaning and purpose in three primary ways: through their possessions (the things that money can buy), through pleasure (the things that bring temporary satisfaction), and through power (the things that make us feel important). Solomon in his book entitled, <u>Ecclesiastes</u>, describes how he fully engaged himself in all three and found that they failed to provide what he was really looking for in life. He did not find lasting satisfaction in them. (Although he may have enjoyed the attempt and many others are enjoying the attempt.)

C.S. Lewis was right when he said, "All your life an unattainable ecstasy has hovered just beyond the grasp of your consciousness. The day is coming when you will wake to find, beyond all hope, that you have attained it, or else, that it was within your reach and you have lost it forever." [12] In other words, the search for meaning and

---

[12] C.S. Lewis, *The Problem of Pain*, (New York: Macmillan, 1962), 147.

purpose is within our grasp.

In one of the most ancient books, the book of Psalms, Moses writes in the 90th Psalm about the brevity of life and the eternity of God. He compares the passing of life to the growth of new grass, to the changing of the guard, to the passing of a flood. All of these examples are quick, fast, and furious. That is a perfect description of life; quick, fast and furious. He states that we have 70 years and maybe 80 if we are lucky. Which ties in pretty closely to the life insurance longevity tables for the life of an American and for the majority of people in the world. Of course, we know that many others die much younger and a few others later.

Moses talks about bringing permanence to the work of his hands. He wants his works to be longer lasting beyond his own life span. I will expand on that a little bit later.

We search for meaning and purpose of life, because we all know in our hearts that there must be something deeper, stronger, and more everlasting than eating, drinking, sleeping, and working. There must be something more than hours on the internet, text messaging, or even enjoying music on our iPhone. There must be something more than bonuses from work, vacations in Florida, and NASCAR. There must be something more than paying taxes, playing cards, and pumping gas. There is something deep within the human soul that speaks to us, that there is something else out there. Do the X-Files really hold the secret?

Pascal said, "All men seek happiness. This is without exception. Whatever different means they employ, they all tend to this end." [13] We are all in that pursuit of the elusive happiness that brings us purpose and meaning.

What is out there? Better yet, who is out there? Part of the answer to this big question revolves around the existence of God. To me it is God who brings us meaning and purpose of life. It is God who can make the works of our hands permanent. It is God who gives a reason for living and a reason to share our lives and possessions for the benefit of others.

---

[13] Blaise Pascal, *Pensees*, trans. W.F. Trotter, Christian Classics Ethereal Library, http://www.ccel.org/p/pascal/pensees/cache/pensees.pdf , section vii, article 425.

Why God? But maybe more important, who is God? This is a rather big question. Simply stated, God is spirit. God is eternal. God is love. God is good. There are hundreds of words that describe the attributes of the God of the Bible. We cannot see God. However, God is out there. He is our creator. He is our giver of life. He gives purpose and meaning. He gives us a reason to live.

I believe that Jesus is God. How could he be God? He was a carpenter, born in a remote town of Israel. Could he be God?

Imagine if a farmer made a decision to flood his field with water. As he makes the necessary preparations, he notices an anthill that would be washed away by the waters. How could the farmer best warn the ants of their impending doom? He could make a sign and post it. He could holler and scream. He could send them a text message. He could make an announcement on the radio, but they would never understand. The best way for the farmer to warn the ants, would be if he would become an ant. Then the farmer could warn them of the danger of the waters that would soon be coming. He could communicate with them in their language. This, in simple terms, describes the incarnation.

Incarnation means in the English "to be incarnate" or "to put on flesh." "Carn" is the root word for flesh in Latin. (Thus, carnivorous animals are meat eaters!) God put on human flesh. God became a man. God was born through a young woman, Mary. He became a man in order to communicate to us the meaning and purpose of life.

Solomon in the book of Ecclesiastes implies that if there is no God then let us eat, drink, and be merry for tomorrow we die. However, there is a God. That God is revealed through Jesus Christ. Do you know him? He will give you meaning and purpose for your life.

Jesus made this astounding statement, "I have come that they might have life and that they might have it abundantly." Not only life, but abundant life. Can you think of anything more wonderful? You can find the meaning and purpose of life in Him! How? By simply trusting Him as your Savior. He died for your sins on the cross. By faith in Him we can have our sins forgiven. He then gives us the gift of salvation.

He gives us the gift of Eternal Life. Eternal Life is where meaning and purpose is found through our relationship with Christ.

Chapter 17

The Big Question
What is the Sovereignty of God?

This question always seems to result in a debate between the sovereignty of God and the free will of man. The purpose of this essay is to focus on God's sovereignty and not to "solve" the debate.

The word "sovereign" in the Greek New Testament is the word <u>dunastes</u>. (Our English word "dynasty" has its origins in this word.) This word means a ruler, a potentate, a lord, or master. The root of the word comes from the Greek word for power, <u>dunamai</u>. This word means to be able or to have power. Our English word "dynamo" or "dynamite" has its origins in this word.

This word "sovereign" appears in 1 Timothy 6:15, where Paul says, *"He who is the blessed and only Sovereign, the King of Kings and Lord of Lords."* He is describing Jesus, as the Sovereign King and Lord of the universe. Jesus is the ruler, master, and Lord. He has authority over all the universe. He has power over the universe.

The Merriam-Webster's Collegiate Dictionary defines "sovereign" as: 1) one possessing or held to possess sovereignty 2) one that exercises supreme authority within a limited sphere 3) an acknowledged leader.

Chip Ingram says this about the word "sovereign," "If you were to look up the word 'sovereign' in the dictionary, you would find words and phrases like 'superior,' 'greatest,' 'supreme in power and authority,' 'ruler,' and 'independent of all others.' But the way I like to explain God's sovereignty best is simply to say, 'God is in control.' There is absolutely nothing that happens in the universe that is outside of God's influence and authority. As King of Kings and Lord of Lords, God has no limitations."[14]

In the Theopedia (An Encyclopedia of Christianity) the sovereignty of God is defined in this way. "The **Sovereignty of God** is the biblical teaching that all things are under God's rule and control, and that nothing happens without His direction or permission. God works not just some

---

[14] http://www.christianity.com/christian foundations/theological faq

things but all things according to the counsel of His own will (see Eph. 1:11). His purposes are all-inclusive and never thwarted (see Isa. 46:11); nothing takes Him by surprise. The sovereignty of God is not merely that God has the power and right to govern all things, but that He does so, always and without exception. In other words, God is not merely sovereign *de jure* (in principle), but sovereign *de facto* (in practice)."[15]

    A.W. Pink has written a book entitled, The Sovereignty of God, he says, "What do we mean by [the sovereignty of God]? We mean the supremacy of God, the kingship of God, the godhood of God. To say that God is Sovereign is to declare that God is God. To say that God is Sovereign is to declare that He is the Most High, doing according to His will in the army of Heaven, and among the inhabitants of the earth, so that none can stay His hand or say unto Him what doest Thou? (Dan. 4:35). To say that God is Sovereign is to declare that He is the Almighty, the Possessor of all power in Heaven and earth, so that none can defeat His counsels, thwart His purpose, or resist His will (Psa. 115:3). To say that

---

[15] http://www.theopedia.com/Sovereignty_of_God

God is Sovereign is to declare that He is "The Governor among the nations" (Psa. 22:28), setting up kingdoms, overthrowing empires, and determining the course of dynasties as pleaseth Him best. To say that God is Sovereign is to declare that He is the "Only Potentate, the King of kings, and Lord of lords" (1 Tim. 6:15). Such is the God of the Bible."[16]

    All these authors seem to be saying the same thing, the sovereignty of God means that God is in control of the universe. Jesus is declared as King of Kings and Lord of Lords. Let's look at three examples from the bible that illustrate God's sovereignty.

    The first is from the life of Joseph in the book of Genesis. I'm sure you are familiar with the story. Joseph is one of the 12 sons of Jacob. He wears the coat of many colors. He is a dreamer. His dreams seem to lift himself up above his father, mother, and brothers. Soon his brothers become embittered and hateful towards him. Joseph eventually ends up as a slave in Egypt. Through a series of amazing "circumstances," Joseph becomes second in

---

[16] A. W. Pink, *The Sovereignty of God*, chapter 1.

command of all of Egypt, just under the Pharaoh. His position of power allows his family and nation to survive the severe famine. I want to focus on what Joseph said about his brothers and his circumstances. What he says illustrates the sovereign hand of God. In Genesis 50:19-21 Joseph says to his brothers after the death of their father, *"But Joseph said to them, 'Do not be afraid, for am I in God's place? As for you, you meant evil against me, but God meant it for good in order to bring about this present result, to preserve many people alive. So therefore, do not be afraid; I will provide for you and your little ones.' So he comforted them and spoke kindly to them."*

    Joseph is declaring that God was sovereign in his personal circumstances. He was declaring that God was in control. He was saying that God used what was intended for evil to be turned into something good. This could only happen if God was in control.

    The second example is also from the Old Testament. It is from the book of Chronicles. In 2 Chronicles 18: 28-34 we read the story of the death of wicked King Ahab, the King of Israel. The kings of Israel and Judah went to war against

Ramoth-gilead. The king of Israel disguised himself so he wouldn't be killed in battle thinking he would be safe. The army of Ramoth-gilead goes after the King of Judah, Jehoshaphat. *"When the captains of the chariots saw that it was not the king of Israel, they turned back from pursuing him. A certain man drew his bow at random and struck the king of Israel in a joint of the armor. So he said to the driver of the chariot, "Turn around and take me out of the fight, for I am severely wounded." The battle raged that day, and the king of Israel propped himself up in his chariot in front of the Arameans until the evening; and at sunset he died."*

    Several things strike me from this passage. The first is that man can plan his steps, but the Lord determines the outcome. King Ahab thought he could avoid the battle through his disguise, but God brings the battle to him anyway. The second is the "random" arrow that is shot in the air. It just "happens" to strike the king in the joint of the armor. What are the chances for a random arrow to hit the precise point of separation of the pieces of armor? King Ahab is killed. God wanted this evil king of Israel killed and removed from office.

This was the method that God had chosen to use. There are no "random" acts. God is in control.

A third example comes from the New Testament. It is found in Peter's first sermon at Pentecost in the second chapter of the book of Acts. *"Men of Israel, listen to these words: Jesus the Nazarene, a man attested to you by God with miracles and wonders and signs which God performed through Him in your midst, just as you yourselves know—this Man, delivered over by the predetermined plan and foreknowledge of God, you nailed to a cross by the hands of godless men and put Him to death. But God raised Him up again, putting an end to the agony of death, since it was impossible for Him to be held in its power."*

This sermon is directed to the men of Judea and all who live in Jerusalem. It is directed towards the religious leaders who put Jesus to death at the hands of Pilate. Three things intrigue me in this passage. Peter mentions 1) the predetermined plan of God, 2) the foreknowledge of God, and 3) the personal responsibility of the religious leaders for the crucifixion of Christ. In this one verse Peter seems to be putting these three concepts together. The first is that God was always in control. What happened to Jesus happened because God allowed it. It was part of his predetermined plan. Secondly, the fact that Jesus was put to death did not surprise God. When Jesus died, God did not say, "Oh no, what am I going to do now?" There was no surprise. God knew in advance that it would happen. Finally, God still held the religious leaders accountable for the death of Jesus. Peter says to them, "You nailed to the cross by the hands of godless men." They had put Jesus to death. They were responsible. They would give an account of this action to God.

These three examples help us to see the meaning of the sovereignty of God. God is always in control. Nothing happens anywhere in the universe apart from his control. From the death of a sparrow to the explosion of a super nova in the heavens, nothing happens in the universe or on earth apart from the sovereign hand of God.

"The LORD has established His throne in the heavens, And His sovereignty rules over all." Psalm 103:19

Discussion Questions:

1. Define the phrase "sovereignty of God" in your own words.

2. Does anything <u>comfort</u> you about knowing that God is in control?

3. Does anything <u>trouble</u> you about knowing that God is in control?

4. Describe a situation or circumstance from your own life where you could see the "sovereignty of God" in action.

5. How can you bring the gospel message into the truth of the sovereignty of God?

Chapter 18

The Big Question
When will Jesus return?

This is a question that has intrigued people for ages. Throughout history, since Jesus left the earth, people have wondered when He would return. Dates have been set. Prophecies have been studied, but no return of Jesus. I remember in 1988 coming out of church one day and finding on my car a flier entitled, "88 Reasons why Jesus will return in 1988." Of course, that didn't happen or else I missed His return.

In recent days there has been lots of discussion of the year 2012 because of an indication on the Mayan calendar of a cataclysmic event predicted for December 21, 2012. See the online article from USA Today: (http://www.usatoday.com/tech/science/2007-03-27-maya-2012_N.htm) This Mayan prediction was made over 5,000 years ago!

However, the real origin of the question began on the day that Jesus ascended into heaven

40 days after His resurrection. The disciples asked Jesus, "Lord, is it at this time You are restoring the kingdom to Israel. (Hoping for the Messiah King to come and deliver them from the Romans.) Read the words of Luke in Acts 1:6-11 from the New Testament: *So when they had come together, they asked him, "Lord, will you at this time restore the kingdom to Israel?" He said to them, "It is not for you to know times or seasons that the Father has fixed by his own authority. But you will receive power when the Holy Spirit has come upon you, and you will be my witnesses in Jerusalem and in all Judea and Samaria, and to the end of the earth." And when he had said these things, as they were looking on, he was lifted up, and a cloud took him out of their sight. And while they were gazing into heaven as he went, behold, two men stood by them in white robes, and said, "Men of Galilee, why do you stand looking into heaven? This Jesus, who was taken up from you into heaven, will come in the same way as you saw him go into heaven."*

    Notice that Jesus tells them that they were not to know "the times or seasons that the Father had fixed."

The problem is that the time of His return is never mentioned. The disciples thought it would be immediate. He has delayed His return for almost 2,000 years. Could the Mayans be right?

The Scriptures indicate that the Mayans are wrong. Here is what we find in the New Testament:

Matthew 24:36

*"But concerning that day and hour **no one knows**, not even the angels of heaven, nor the Son, but the Father only.*

Matthew 24:42

*Therefore, stay awake, for **you do not know** on what day your Lord is coming.*

Matthew 24:44

*Therefore, you also must be ready, for the Son of Man is coming at an hour **you do not expect**.*

Matthew 24:50

*the master of that servant will come on a day when he does not expect him and at **an hour he does not know***

Matthew 25:13

*Watch therefore, for **you know neither the day nor the hour**.*

1 Thessalonians 5:2-3

*For you yourselves are fully aware that the day of the Lord will come **like a thief** in the night. While people are saying, "There is peace and security," then sudden destruction will come upon them as labor pains come upon a pregnant woman, and they will not escape.*

The exact day and hour of His return has not been revealed. All of these Scriptures seem to indicate that the return of the Lord will come suddenly, and un-expectantly. It will come on a day and hour that is least expected. It will come like a thief in the night. If a thief wants to break into your house, he doesn't announce the day of the month or the hour. He comes when you least expect it. (Or he waits until you are at a neighborhood watch meeting.)

However, I must say a few words about signs that accompany the Lord's return. Also, I must say that all of these remarks are concerning the Second Coming of Christ and not the Rapture of the Church. The Rapture of the Church is a completely different discussion for a later date.

In the 24th chapter of the gospel of Matthew there are signs described that would accompany the return of the Lord. You can find at least 10 different signs in this chapter. These signs do not reveal the day nor hour of His return, but they do indicate when we see the signs that we should be preparing for His eminent return.

We read the following in verse 3:
As he sat on the Mount of Olives, the disciples came to him privately, saying, "Tell us, when will these things be, and what will be the sign of your coming and of the end of the age?"

Signs are indicators. Signs point the way to

something. If we are driving down the interstate, we will see a sign that says the next rest stop is 50 miles away. That sign gives us an indication of how close we are to the next rest stop. The signs surrounding the Second Coming of Christ are similar. When we see the signs, we know that His return is near.

Matthew 24:33-34 says, *"So also, when you see all these things, you know that he is near, at the very gates. Truly, I say to you, this generation will not pass away until all these things take place."* There has been lots of discussion by evangelicals on the word, "generation."

What does Matthew mean by "this generation?" The Greek word for "generation" is genea. This word is often translated race, family, or generation. It is the root word of our English word, genealogy. The word genea comes from the Greek word, ginomai, which means to come into being. Generation means people of the same kind or descendants. The word "this" in the Greek is houtos. This word means this or this one. It designates the nearer of two things.

What Matthew seems to be saying is that when the reader sees all the signs being fulfilled, then he can know that the Lord's return is near. Again, the day and hour are not revealed. We are to be alert ready for His return. (Read the parable of the Ten Virgins in Matthew 25:1-13 and the parable of the Talents in Matthew 25:14-30.) The generation that sees these signs being fulfilled will witness the Lord's return.

Are we the generation that will witness the Lord's return? Will you be ready for His return? Have you trusted in Christ as your Lord and Savior and coming King? If you are a believer, are you walking in obedience to Him, sharing the gospel with all who will listen? Are you making disciples?

Chapter 19

The Big Question
Why are There so Many Hypocrites in the Church?

First of all isn't it great that the hypocrites are in the church and not out on the streets. The church is probably a great place for the hypocrites to be.

I need to begin with a couple of definitions, namely, what is the church and what is a hypocrite?

What is the church? The church is the "called out ones." The Greek word is "ecclesia" which means literally those called out. The church is composed of believers that have been called out of the world. There is the church universal, which is composed of all believers. Believers of all denominations are part of the church universal. Believers who have a common faith in Jesus Christ are also part of the church universal. Then there is the local church. The local church is composed of believers who attend worship in a building at a

Sunday gathering. In the USA there are thousands of such churches of hundreds of denominations that gather every Sunday. (and a few on Saturday.) In Johnson City, TN where I live, there are over 200 churches that serve a population of 65,000. There are literally churches on every street corner. You could go to a different church every Sunday and do it for four years.

What are hypocrites? The Greek word for "hypocrite" means "actor." A hypocrite was an actor. A hypocrite was someone who pretended to be someone else. They had a different persona. They lived a double life. An example of this would be someone who says publicly that they oppose the consumption of alcohol, yet privately drink at home. Or the person, who publicly talks about marital fidelity, yet is having an affair with his secretary. A hypocrite says one thing, but does another.

Jesus had a lot to say about hypocrites. He condemned them quite severely. He challenges the hypocrite to be true to themselves. In the book of Revelation, he makes the case that being lukewarm is much more damaging than being hot or cold. You end up spewing out the lukewarm.

Unfortunately, there are many believers in that category. The hypocrite is the one with one foot in the world and the other foot in heaven. They are always straddling the line. They are always inching close to temptation and seeing how far they can go without falling or being caught.

How did Jesus do in choosing his friends? Some people would even say that whom you choose as friends reflects your personal character. Well, it is interesting to read the description of the friends of Jesus. Jesus was the friend of tax-gatherers and sinners. His enemies would often "throw this in his face." "If you are the Son of God, then wouldn't you know the character of this woman who is anointing your feet?" Tax-gatherers were some of the most despised people in Israel. They collected taxes for the Romans from their fellow Jews. Of course, they skimmed a little off the top for this is how they were paid. The "sinners" were those living in disobedience to the Mosaic Law. They were the prostitutes, the lawbreakers, the Sabbath breakers, the rule breakers, and the rebellious. The tax-gatherers and the sinners were the very people that Jesus came to save. These were the types of people who responded to his message of grace, mercy, and forgiveness.

Several years ago, a lesbian couple attended our church. This caused quite a stir in our congregation. How could they be permitted to stay? Why did they feel comfortable in attending the services? Why doesn't someone in authority do something? The elders were contacted and "encouraged" to deal with this "problem." However, I had a completely different "take" on the situation. I was glad they were in attendance. This meant that somehow, they were feeling the love of Christ and not the condemnation of others. It is *in* the church that lives are changed and convictions are reversed.

In a similar vein, one day I received a phone call that members of our college group on campus had been getting drunk on weekends and attending our CRU meetings on Thursdays. My reaction was "praise the Lord." This meant that these young men and women felt free to come to the place where their lives could be changed and new convictions put into place. Were we hypocrites in allowing them to attend. No. Of course not. Jesus came to heal the sick. Only the sick need a physician. When you are healthy, you do not need a physician. Now those that were living this "double life" were not leaders in our movement. They did not lead worship. They were forgiven sinners like all the rest of us.

Where the real issue of hypocrisy comes into play is when someone is saying one thing and completely doing another. Using the drinking example, the person who says that all alcohol is sin, but drinks on the weekends is a hypocrite and should be challenged on it. The person who says that all movies are wrong, but attends them regularly is a hypocrite. The person who opposes "mixed bathing" but spends hours looking at internet pornography is a hypocrite.

The Pharisees, the religious leaders of their day, were hypocrites. They said one thing but lived another. They said they stood for mercy and justice, but they condemned an innocent man to death. They said they loved and followed Jehovah, but their actions and attitudes contradicted their words and affirmations. They were hypocrites.

Why are there hypocrites in the church? Because the church is composed of forgiven, but fallen people. The church is composed of hypocrites, because we are all hypocrites to one degree to another. How many of us truly and fully adhere to everything we claim to believe? There is no one who is 100% consistent. We are all hypocrites.

The difference is that the Lord wants us to confess our sins and to live consistently according to his word. When we fail, we should admit it. When we act differently than what we claim to believe, then we should confess it. When we are inconsistent in our behavior, we should repent and do it differently.

Yes. There are hypocrites in the church, but thank God, they are in the church. We would hate to have them running around the streets.

Chapter 20

The Big Question
Why do Bad things happen to Good people?

Why do bad things happen to good people? That is a very good question to consider. It is a question that many people desire an answer for. I wonder if other religions are seeking an answer or is it only Christianity?

In our world, it is true. Bad things happen to good people. Innocent babies are aborted every day. Infants are born blind. Good-hearted people are killed in car crashes. Teenagers are caught in riptides and drown. Cancer strikes the good of heart. The innocent man is murdered. The life savings of the generous couple are down the drain with all the other Wall Street investments.

Maybe it would be good to identify the terms "bad" and "good." What do we mean by "bad?" I guess we normally mean those things that are not good. We mean things that bring sadness. Things that break relationships. Things that cause death or injury. The unexpected setback. The illness that is terminal. The life that is difficult. The marriage that is broken. Yes. All these things are bad.

What is good? Good is what is pure, holy, and kind. Goodness is what we enjoy. It is what is right, true, and affirming. When a child is good, they are obedient. When a teenager is good, they call their parents if they are running late in the evening. A husband is good when he provides for his family and loves his wife and children unconditionally. A wife is good when she cares and nurtures her family and creates a home of love. A person is good when they share generously with others. The giver is good when he gives the anonymous gift.

This brings us back to our question: why do bad things happen to good people? Part of the answer is that some things in life are really out of our control. (Is there really anything that is under our "control"?) We cannot control the weather. We cannot control the stock market. We cannot control who gets cancer. We cannot control the earthquake, tidal wave, or rip tide. We cannot control the final score of the game we are watching. In other words, most of the things that go bad are out of our control.

If we were really students of this, we would probably discover that bad things also happen to bad people. Moreover, that that is probably more often the case. Incredibly bad things happen to bad people. However, that does not help answer our question very well.

However, I think it also is important to consider that incredibly good things also happen to good people. The generous person is often blessed by their generosity. The kind person often receives kindness in return. The forgiving person experiences personal forgiveness in a deeper way. The merciful person knows what true mercy is all about. The humble person is often exalted.

Now let us bring God into the equation. The living God, the God of Abraham, Isaac, and Jacob. The God who really cares for us and proved it by sending his son to earth, Jesus Christ. In the book of Romans, we read, "And God causes all things to work together for good to those who love God, to those who are called according to His purpose." Notice what this verse is not saying. It is not saying that all things that happen are good. It is saying that God can make all things work *together* for good. The verse also does not say that we will understand why bad things happen. No explanation is ever offered. We may not ever know why bad things happen. However, we can be assured that God can make some good out of it. Somehow, someway, He can make good out of the bad. Often times in life, it is the bad and difficult things that make us stronger. The bad things can build our character. The challenging things can strengthen our faith. As we grow older, we can look back and see how the hard and tough things have made us into the man or woman that we are today. Would any growth happen apart from these bad things?

      Now, in my opinion I would rather avoid the pain. However, there is no newborn baby apart from the pain of childbirth. The wisdom tooth cannot be removed unless the tooth is painfully extracted. The athlete will never grow stronger unless his muscles are toughened, stretched, and exercised. The oyster will never produce the pearl, unless it heals the flesh around the painful grain of sand.

Why do bad things happen to good people? Because life can be hard, difficult, and tough. No rose garden has ever been promised. We may not ever know the answer to this question, but it does not change the character of God.

God is always good. God is always kind. God is always merciful. God is always sovereign. God never changes. We can trust God even in the midst of the difficult and painful passages of our lives.

To read what the Bible says about suffering of the innocent read the book of Job and the book of Lamentations.

Chapter 21

The Big Question
Why is there Evil and Suffering in the world?

First, we have to accept the basic premise that there is evil and suffering in the world. If you do, then you must define what it is. However, who or what determines the definition? Who sets the boundaries of right or wrong? What gives me pleasure may cause you pain. This would beg the question "are there moral absolutes?" This would be a "Big Question" for another discussion.

I would define suffering as anything that causes pain in our lives. This pain may be physical, emotional, or psychological. The religious may indicate Spiritual pain—the pain of falling short of God's standards.

Evil is a little harder to define. The opposite of evil is good. The Apostle Paul describes good as that which is the will of God for our live---"that which is good, acceptable, and perfect." Therefore, evil would be that which befalls our lives as being bad, unacceptable, and less than perfect.

There is no doubt that we have all experienced various degrees of evil and suffering in our lives. Sometimes whole nations, cultures, or ethnic groups can experience it. The Jewish people suffered greatly under Nazi Germany. The Kurds experienced near elimination at the hands of Saddam Hussein. Under Pol Pot the Cambodians experienced unspeakable torture, murder, and abuse. Almost 2 million were murdered. Much of it photographed and recorded by the authorities.

Therefore, we have established the fact that evil and suffering exists in our world. In our world, there are two basic worldviews. The first says that the people are basically good and will become better and better. This view holds that given time our world is becoming a better and better place to live in. This should result in less crime, less murder, less abusiveness, less evil and suffering. However, is that the reality?

The second view is radically different. This view holds that man started out good but has become fallen and corrupted. Because of the fallen-ness of man, his heart has become corrupted. This corrupted heart is the cause of much of the evil and suffering in this world. This view is saying that the world and the people in it are not increasingly becoming better and better, rather they are becoming more and more corrupt and generating more and more evil and suffering. This corrupted heart is in need of redemption, but that is for the latter part of this essay.

    I think there are three basic answers to the Big Question of "Why is there evil and suffering in the world?" The first answer is that much of the evil and suffering in this world is the result of our own doing. Much of it is self-inflicted. If a person gets drunk, and crashes his car and injures himself in the wreck, it is a direct result of his choice to drink to excess and to drive under the influence. No one else is responsible for his pain except himself. (Of course, the bartender may have continued to supply drinks even though the person was already drunk. That is getting ahead of myself.) If a person is warned that his excess weight and high levels of cholesterol will eventually result in a heart attack, and he continues to over eat fatty foods and refuses to exercise or diet. His heart attack (in that case) is a direct result of his own choices. If a young boy is told not to play with matches, but he does and then burns himself. His pain is a direct consequence of his disobedience to his parent's instruction. The suffering is a result of his choice.

The second answer to the "Big Question" is that much of the evil and suffering in the world is a result of the choices of others who inflict pain upon our lives. The abusive employer who torments his employees. The teenager who mercilessly ridicules the "outcast" student in his high school. The child predator that uses children to satisfy his lust. This is evil and suffering that is inflicted upon us by others. Look at the history of war and conflicts throughout the world. Wars have been fought over religion, oil, power, and greed. People steal because you have something that they lack and want. People murder over their own anger or rage. People rape the innocent to satisfy their lust and sexual urges. People hate because of the color of their skin.

The final answer to the question to the "Big Question" may be a little less satisfying. How do we explain the apparent "random" acts of evil and suffering that are experienced by the innocent? (Of course, the "guilty" are more deserving of the evil and suffering and maybe rightly so.)

How do you explain the innocent young man who is struck and killed by the stray bullet in a police shoot out at a robbery? I guess you could blame that on the robbers. How do you explain the missionary mother who contracts AIDS from a blood transfusion in an African hospital? Or the young bride who drowns in a rip tide at the beach on her honeymoon? On a little more humorous note, how do you explain the falling coconut, which strikes the head of the vacationer and kills him on the spot. And the examples can be repeated many fold. The simple answer is that there is no answer which is very satisfying at all. The fact is that sometimes evil and suffering happens with no real explanation. There is a mystery to life that can't often be explained.

Which brings me back to redemption. Paul in the book of Romans says, "All things work together for the good for those who love God." Note that he does not say that all things are good. He says that somehow all things work together for the good. As I have said, there is a mystery attached to this. It does not fully answer the question "why." God can make these things work together for the good. As a believer in Christ, I believe that the heart is corrupted and fallen because of sin. Sin is falling short of God's standards and holiness. Because of our sin, we need redemption, which requires a redeemer. Jesus Christ claimed to be that redeemer. His death on the cross was the place of ultimate evil and suffering. An innocent man died for all that is bad in this world. The cross made redemption possible for all.

When we trust him for forgiveness of sins, he forgives us cleanses us and renews us. We become forgiven. Trust in Christ today. He can give you his peace in the midst of the evil and suffering that are in this fallen and painful world.

Made in the USA
Columbia, SC
24 September 2022